**PERSONAL &
FAMILY SAFETY
& CRIME
PREVENTION**

Other Preventive Medicine Institute/Strang Clinic
HEALTH ACTION PLANS

 How to Stop Smoking

 **Nutrition**

 Physical Fitness

PERSONAL & FAMILY SAFETY & CRIME PREVENTION

A Preventive Medicine Institute/Strang Clinic
HEALTH ACTION PLAN

NANCY Z. OLSON, M.P.S.
Health Education Division
PMI/Strang Clinic

Series Editor
Daniel G. Miller, M.D.

Associate Editors
Marilyn Snyder Halper, M.P.H.
Pamela Hatch
Ira Neiger

Holt, Rinehart and Winston   New York

Copyright © 1980 by Preventive Medicine Institute/Strang Clinic

First published in January 1981 by Holt, Rinehart and Winston,
383 Madison Avenue, New York, New York 10017.

Published simultaneously in Canada by Holt, Rinehart and
Winston of Canada, Limited.

Library of Congress Cataloging in Publication Data

Olson, Nancy Z
  Personal and family safety and crime prevention

  (A Preventive Medicine Institute/Strang Clinic
health action plan)
  Includes index.
    1. Accidents—Prevention. 2. Home accidents—
Prevention. 3. Crime prevention. I. Title.
II. Series: Preventive Medicine Institute/Strang
Clinic. Preventive Medicine Institute/Strang Clinic
health action plan.
HV675.044   363.1'37   80-11549

ISBN Hardbound: 0-03-048271-2
ISBN Paperback: 0-03-048266-6

First Edition

Designer: Betty Binns Graphics
Printed in the United States of America
10 9 8 7 6 5 4 3 2 1

Contents

2126969

Foreword

After more than four years of research, study, and testing, it is with great pride and pleasure that we bring you this Preventive Medicine Institute/Strang Clinic Health Action Plan. The development of this book (one of four currently available) has been one of the most exciting—and, we believe, successful—projects the clinic has ever undertaken. By making use of the Health Action Plans, you will be taking a major step toward improving your own health as well as that of your family.

Taken together, these plans address the health problems—cancer, heart disease, and accidents—responsible for the majority of chronic illnesses, disabilities, and premature deaths in this country. The four books—*Personal and Family Safety and Crime Prevention, How to Stop Smoking, Nutrition,* and *Physical Fitness*—deal directly with the behaviors most closely associated with these health concerns.

Until recently, it has been generally assumed that advanced technology, more physicians and better medical care would ensure the health and increase the life spans of most Americans. While we have made tremendous progress in the fields of disease detection and cure, and life expectancy has increased dramatically since the turn of the century, considerable evidence indicates that we have reached a point of diminishing returns. Life expectancy has leveled off in the last few decades, and disease patterns have changed. Infectious diseases such as tuberculosis, pneumonia, and typhoid, once among the most feared health problems, have, for the most part, been replaced by chronic disorders such as cancer and heart disease.

The path to the control of chronic diseases lies in a new direction. While we don't have all the answers, we do have hard evidence that links cancer to smoking, implicates high-fat diets and obesity in cancer and heart disease, and suggests that lack of regular exercise contributes to heart and respiratory problems.

To put it another way, the major causes of chronic disease, disability, and death in the Western world have one important thing in common: they are all connected to some extent to our behavior, our habits. Improved health, therefore, unquestionably will depend upon our ability to throw away our cigarettes, change our dietary habits, exercise regularly, and learn to take precautions against avoidable accidents. In today's world, health depends more on our ability to *prevent* diseases and accidents than on our ability to treat their effects once they have occurred. And since the decision to live wisely is an individual's choice, your health, to a great extent, is in your own hands.

Our belief in the concept of preventive medicine led us to develop the Health Action Plans. Many reputable books on related subjects are available, but we believe ours are unique for three reasons. First, their ultimate objective is *permanent* change in everyday health habits and life-styles. Second, each Health Action Plan provides a *structured* approach to behavioral change—a simple, step-by-step way to achieve personal health-related goals. Third, the structure is similar in each of the Health Action Plans, so if you use one, you will find the format of the others familiar, allowing you to readily develop your own *individualized and integrated* programs.

Each book includes a section on self-assessment to give you a deeper understanding of your current habits. Once you have been made aware of the details of these habits, you are given suggestions for making health-improving changes as well as the tools for achieving your specific goals. In addition, each book makes provision for maintaining change once it has been achieved. The maintenance plans often involve record keeping, which not only increases your awareness and knowledge of a health habit, but arms you with additional reinforcement for further change.

All the Health Action Plans were developed with the help of consultants and consumers. People like you were asked to test each plan and to make suggestions. These consumers were discriminating critics, and their contributions benefited the plans greatly. Health consultants—doctors, nutritionists, exercise physiologists, and other experts—have also carefully considered each program, commenting on content and accuracy and helping in program testing.

None of these plans provides an instant answer: rather, they are personally focused programs for modifying the way you live so that you and your family can enjoy long, happy—and healthy lives.

A person's health must ultimately be his or her own responsibility. We hope that these Health Action Plans will provide you with a practical and reliable guide to a healthier life.

Daniel G. Miller, M.D.
Director, Preventive Medicine
Institute/Strang Clinic

A word about the Preventive Medicine Institute/Strang Clinic

The Preventive Medicine Institute/Strang Clinic is a nonprofit organization dedicated to the prevention of cancer, heart disease, stroke, and other serious illnesses. Established at Memorial Hospital in New York City in 1940 by Dr. Elise Strang L'Esperance, the Strang Clinic originally became well known for its pioneering use of the Pap test, the screening technique for cervical cancer devised by Dr. George Papanicolaou. In 1963 the clinic became an independent center. At that time the clinic—which until then had been devoted largely to cancer detection— broadened its scope to cover diagnosis, research, and detection of all the major chronic and controllable diseases. In 1966 the clinic was renamed the Preventive Medicine Institute/Strang Clinic, with the Strang Clinic serving as the clinical division and the institute serving as the research center.

During the past ten years, the focus of the clinic's work has again widened, emphasizing health education and the role of the individual in preventing disease. In this respect, its goal has been to devise lifelong health and safety programs that deter the onset of disease and injury.

Acknowledgments

The staff of the Preventive Medicine Institute/Strang Clinic would like to thank the following consultants for their assistance and valuable suggestions:

Leslie Fisher
Advisor for Product Safety
New York State Department of Health
Albany, New York

James F. Hughes
Director, General Education Division
New Jersey State Safety Council
Newark, New Jersey

Lucille Niebur
President
Emergency Skills, Inc.
New York, New York

Anne L. Pavlich, R.N., M.N.A.
Consumer Education Program Specialist
U.S. Consumer Product Safety Commission
Washington, D.C.

Kenneth R. Rashid
Acting Director, Office of Communications
U.S. Consumer Product Safety Commission
Washington, D.C.

Captain Donald J. Roberts
Commanding Officer
Crime Prevention Section
New York City Police Department
New York, New York

We also wish to acknowledge the contributions of Wendy Seda, Preventive Medicine Institute/Strang Clinic.

Introduction

Accidents are the leading cause of death among people from one to forty-four years old and ranks behind only cardiovascular disease and cancer. as a killer of people of all ages. Although we tend to think of people as *victims* of accidents or crimes, if we look closely, we find in most cases that some preventive action could have been taken. Not all accidents or incidents of crime are avoidable, of course, but lack of preparation only increases the risk.

This Preventive Medicine Institute/Strang Clinic Health Action Plan, *Personal and Family Safety and Crime Prevention,* is designed to help you and members of your family recognize hazardous conditions in your home, at your place of employment, in your car, and while at play. In a simple, step-by-step manner, you create a personal safety checklist that helps you pinpoint spots in both your environment and your behavior where safety measures are inadequate. Once you are aware of these areas of inadequacy, you can begin to correct them.

The program works like this. At the beginning of each chapter, you will find a self-assessment of safety points pertaining to the subject of that chapter. Read the list and answer yes or no to each question. In a notebook or on a sheet of paper, copy word for word each question to which you've answered no. When you have done this for each self-assessment, you will have a checklist of areas where your personal attention to safety might be improved. Then it is up to you to act.

The text of *Personal and Family Safety and Crime Prevention* describes significant dangers around the house, on the road (either walking or driving), at your place of employment (an office or an industrial plant), and during the most hazardous recreational activities. Directions and suggestions are given to help you alter accident-inviting behavior and change various aspects of your environment to create as danger-free a life as is possible. Refer to your personal lists and then take action to improve safety measures in those areas that apply to you.

Part 1

Safety around the house

CHAPTER 1
Hints for general household safety

Most accidents, with the exception of traffic accidents, occur at home. This may be simply because our homes are where we spend most of our time, and the ratio between time spent and accidents happening is a naturally high one. But very likely, the reason is more complex. We relax in our homes, whereas at work or at play, other people's rules and needs must be taken into account. But here is precisely where the problem begins. At home, the responsibility for safe behavior is ours and ours alone. No one tells us what to do; no one provides rules. It is up to us to create a safe home environment, and often we don't do it, simply because we would rather relax.

In Part 1 of the Health Action Plan, we tackle the problem of making the entire home environment accident-proof. In this first section, we focus on general household safety problems and discuss the most common accidents that can happen in any room. In later sections, we will discuss household areas where accidents occur most frequently.

Begin this section by devising your personal general household safety checklist. On a sheet of notebook paper, write word for word each question in the following self-assessment to which you answered no.

After completing the self-assessment, read the text, which discusses a number of common household accidents and gives advice for avoiding them or for handling them should they occur in your home.

Self-assessment

DO YOU:

	YES	NO
■ Walk through your house once a year deliberately looking for safety hazards?	___	___
■ Avoid carrying loads that block your vision?	___	___
■ Avoid using stairways as temporary storage areas?	___	___
■ Use a flashlight when entering a dark area if a light switch is not within easy reach?	___	___
■ Avoid lifting heavy objects without assistance?	___	___
■ Use a sturdy stepladder for reaching high places?	___	___
■ Store frequently used items in easy-to-reach storage areas?	___	___
■ Always use a screen in front of a fireplace?	___	___
■ Keep lighted candles away from walls and curtains?	___	___
■ Check that matches and cigarettes are completely extinguished before discarding?	___	___
■ Refrain from smoking in bed?	___	___
■ Turn room heaters off at bedtime and whenever you leave the house unattended?	___	___
■ Keep matches and lighters out of the reach of small children?	___	___
■ Store firearms in a locked rack or cabinet?	___	___
■ Store ammunition separately?	___	___
■ Store household poisons, such as cleaning products, out of the reach of children?	___	___
■ Avoid buying paints or other household products that contain lead?	___	___
■ Keep syrup of ipecac in the house in case of accidental poisoning?	___	___
■ Keep a complete first-aid kit in your house?	___	___

	YES	NO

- Check and replenish your first-aid kit at least every six months? _____ _____

- Keep a list of emergency telephone numbers next to your telephone? _____ _____

- Have a strong handrail or bannister placed along each stairway? _____ _____

- Have strong, sufficiently high railings protecting any balcony? _____ _____

- Have safety guardrails on upper-level windows if children are in the house? _____ _____

- Keep stairs, halls, and exits free of clutter? _____ _____

- Keep wood floors, linoleum, and rugs free from rough spots and holes? _____ _____

- Always use slip-resistant floor wax? _____ _____

- Repair frayed electrical cords promptly? _____ _____

- Have good lighting throughout the house, especially in heavily traveled areas such as hallways? _____ _____

- Have light switches at the top and bottom of every staircase? _____ _____

- Have nightlights placed in each bedroom, bathroom, and hall? _____ _____

- Avoid overloading electrical circuits by having several wall outlets? _____ _____

- Have your furniture arranged to allow for easy movement into and around each room? _____ _____

- Have each piece of heavy furniture equipped with casters so it can be moved easily? _____ _____

- Fasten each throw rug to the floor or make sure it is backed with nonskid material? _____ _____

Self-assessment
(continued)

DO YOU:

	YES	NO
■ Avoid running electrical cords under rugs, furniture, or doors, or across a heavily traveled floor space?	___	___
■ Equip all glass doors with safety glass?	___	___
■ Tape or decorate glass doors so they are clearly visible?	___	___
■ Have smoke detectors or similar protective devices to alert family members to fire?	___	___
■ Have at least one fire extinguisher in your house?	___	___
■ Use flame-resistant fabrics for children's sleepwear?	___	___
■ Know how to call the fire department quickly? (And do all members of your family?)	___	___
■ Know how to call the police department quickly? (And do all members of your family?)	___	___
■ Have a fire-escape plan, with alternate routes? (And does each member of the family know what to do?)	___	___
■ Know where your nearest hospital with an emergency room is located?	___	___
■ Know what to do in case of poisoning?	___	___
■ Know basic first aid and how to use a first-aid kit?	___	___
■ Know where to get medical help quickly?	___	___
■ Know what to do if someone is choking?	___	___
■ Know what to do in case of a chemical burn?	___	___
■ Know some of the special accident risks of disabled persons?	___	___
■ Participate in a first-aid course every two years?	___	___
■ Know how to protect children from injuries resulting from toys?	___	___

☐ General first aid

Every adult (and in a family, every adolescent child) should know basic first-aid techniques and be able to apply them quickly. A fall, a heart attack, or a serious cut can happen with lightning speed, and unless first aid is applied with equal speed, serious injury or even death can result. Prepare yourself for emergencies by taking a few simple precautions.

Take a course in first aid every two to five years. Most people think they know what to do if someone chokes or faints, but, in fact, when faced with the real emergency, they freeze. First-aid techniques should be as natural as walking, so that in an emergency you can act with certainty. Most Ys or adult-education centers offer basic first-aid courses, usually for a nominal fee. Check your telephone directory and call your local Y or Red Cross for information.

Post key emergency telephone numbers next to every telephone in your home. These numbers should include those of your physician, your local hospital, an ambulance service, a drugstore, the police and fire departments, a local poison-control center, and a taxi service. Study the form above, and devise one of your own, listing emergency numbers relevant to your personal needs.

Keep a complete first-aid kit in a handy location and replenish it frequently. If you live in a large house, keep a first-aid kit on every floor or in separate areas of the house. For example, you might keep one kit in an upstairs bath, one in the kitchen, and one in a basement workshop. In any case, each family member should know where each first-aid kit is located, should be able to find it quickly, and, of course, should know how to use its contents.

Finally, study the Preventive Medicine Institute/Strang Clinic first-aid chart on the next page. Instructions for treating common household accidents and illnesses are outlined.

This chart has been designed so it can be easily photocopied. Take it to a photocopy store in your town or neighborhood and have several copies made. Post a copy in every medicine cabinet and near every first-

---

EMERGENCY TELEPHONE NUMBERS

Doctor	_____
Poison-control center	_____
Drugstore	_____
Hospital	_____
Ambulance	_____
Fire department	_____
Police department	_____
Taxi	_____
Other numbers	_____
	_____
	_____
	_____
	_____

aid kit in your house. Put copies near other household areas where accidents might be likely to occur—kitchen, bathroom, garage, playroom, or workshop.

☐ **A basic first-aid kit**

SUPPLIES	PURPOSE
Sterile gauze pads	To clean and cover wounds; to use as compresses to stop bleeding
Adhesive bandages in various sizes	To cover minor cuts or scratches
Adhesive tape	To bind gauze or other dressings to the wound
Antiseptic lotion such as tincture of iodine or Merthiolate	To cleanse and disinfect a wound
Calamine lotion	To soothe insect bites, sunburn, and rashes
Syrup of ipecac	To induce vomiting in *some* cases of poisoning
Cotton balls	To apply antiseptic and to clean wounds
Thermometer	To check temperature
Scissors	To cut bandages

First-aid chart

ARTIFICIAL RESPIRATION

Use mouth-to-mouth or mouth-to-nose rescue techniques for a victim of drowning, smoke inhalation, electric shock, heart attack, or any other case where a person stops breathing.

TECHNIQUE

1 Place the victim on his back.

2 Clear the victim's throat by turning his head to the side and with your fingers wiping out any fluid, vomit, or foreign body.

3 Tilt the victim's head back. Extend his neck as far as possible to keep his tongue out of his air passage.

4 Place your mouth tightly over the victim's mouth, pinch his nostrils to prevent air from leaking out, and *blow* into the victim's mouth. (Or, hold the victim's lips closed with your fingers, and breath slowly and steadily into his nose until you see his chest rise.)

5 Remove your mouth and allow the victim's lungs to empty.

6 Repeat with breaths appropriate for the victim's size at a rate of about 15 to 20 breaths per minute. For an infant, use only shallow puffs.

7 Continue the rescue technique until the victim starts to breathe on his own or until a physician arrives.

8 If, after repeated attempts, no air is being exchanged, check that foreign matter is not blocking the victim's air passages. Turn the victim on his side and give several sharp blows between the shoulder blades to jar foreign matter free. Sweep your fingers through the victim's mouth to remove any loose matter.

BITES

ANIMAL BITE
Wash the wound with soap under running water to flush out all dirt and debris. Apply a sterile dressing and then consult a doctor. It may be necessary for the victim to be given tetanus toxoid or antiserum. Always try to capture the animal so it can be tested for rabies.

Note: The incidence of rabies, particularly in domestic animals, is sharply decreasing. It is advisable to have a health department physician involved in any decision regarding administering rabies vaccine.

First-aid chart
(continued)

INSECT BITE
Scrape out the stinger, using a scraping motion of the fingernail. Apply cold compresses to the bitten area. See a doctor immediately if unusual swelling occurs or if the victim feels cold, clammy, or faint.

SNAKE BITE
Nonpoisonous: Wash the bite with soap under running water. Apply sterile gauze dressing.

Poisonous: Keep the victim as inactive as possible. Apply a constricting band above the bite (i.e., between the bite and the victim's heart) and take the victim to a hospital emergency room or a physician as quickly as possible.

BURNS

Immerse the burned area in cold water or apply towels soaked in ice water. For a **severe burn,** keep the victim calm and comfortably warm. Apply cool compresses and take the victim to a physician or a hospital emergency room immediately. Never break blisters. Never apply ointments, grease, or powders.

For a **chemical burn**, wash the burned area thoroughly with water. Consult a physician.

CHOKING

Perform the Heimlich maneuver (see page 14) to dislodge the foreign body. If the victim has stopped breathing, administer artificial respiration and transport him to nearest hospital emergency room. Have someone phone ahead so the hospital can be ready to do emergency surgery if necessary.

CONVULSIONS

Place the victim in a spot where he cannot hurt himself. Apply cold compresses to his head and sponge him with cool water. Do not try to make the patient eat or drink. *Consult a physician immediately.*

CUTS AND SCRAPES

Wash the wound with soap under running water and apply a sterile dressing. For a **large cut**, wash the cut area. Apply the dressing and then apply pressure directly onto the cut area. Elevate the injured part to assist in stopping the bleeding. If bleeding is severe, *proceed to a hospital emergency room*.

EYE INJURIES

To remove a **foreign particle**, use a moist cotton swab to "stroke" the irritated area always toward the outer edges of the eye.

If a **chemical** has gotten into the eye, place the victim on his back and slowly pour fresh water into the corner of the eye to flush out the chemical. *Consult a physician* if irritation to the eye persists and bring the chemical or the label of the container with you.

FAINTING

If a person feels faint, have him sit down and lower his head to his knees. If he becomes unconscious, loosen his clothing and lay him on his back with the legs elevated 3 or 4 inches. If possible, wave smelling salts under his nose. Do not try to force the patient to eat or drink anything. When consciousness returns, keep the patient quiet for at least 15 minutes. If consciousness does not return promptly, *call a physician*.

FRACTURES

If an injured area looks deformed in any way, it usually means that a bone is fractured. *Do not move the victim* if you suspect a fracture of the leg, neck, or back. Call an ambulance for emergency service at once.

FROSTBITE

If an area has been overexposed to the cold, protect the frozen area from further injury by keeping it warm. Keep the frozen area covered with extra clothing and blankets. If the victim is outdoors, bring him indoors immediately. Prepare a warm drink such as tea or cocoa for the victim. Rewarm the frozen area by immersing it in **warm** water, not hot. Do not rub the area, as this may cause gangrene. If blisters appear, do not attempt to break them. Once the affected area has been rewarmed, try to have the victim exercise it. If the affected area includes toes and/or fingers, place dry, sterile gauze between the digits in order to keep them separated.

Call a physician as soon as possible.

First-aid chart
(continued)

HEAT EXHAUSTION

If a person who has been exposed to extreme heat sweats profusely and complains of nausea and headache, chances are he is suffering from heat exhaustion. Give the victim sips of salt water (1 teaspoon of salt per glass, half a glass every 15 minutes), over a 1-hour period. Loosen his clothing and have the victim lie down and raise his feet 8 to 12 inches. Apply wet cloths and fan the victim or move him to an air-conditioned room.

Call a physician as soon as possible.

POISONING

If the poison container is available, use the antidote recommended on the label. If the patient is conscious, *induce vomiting, except* if the victim has swallowed kerosene, gasoline, another petroleum product, lye, or acid. If the poison is unknown, insist that the victim keep drinking large amounts of water.

To induce vomiting, give the victim 1 tablespoon of syrup of ipecac in 1 cup of water. In the absence of ipecac, induced gagging with a finger in the throat may lead to vomiting. Keep the victim's head lower than his hips to prevent choking while vomiting.

Call a physician, poison-control center, or hospital emergency room immediately.

SPRAINS

Elevate the injured area. Apply cold compresses for at least 30 minutes. If swelling is great, the injured limb should not be used until a physician has checked it.

☐ Falls

Falling, the most common single cause of injury around the house, is usually the result of simple carelessness. A fall usually results from something as trivial as a warped rug edge, a neglected toy, a wet floor, or an unnoticed pet. In addition, a fall is likely to occur when you resort to a makeshift climbing apparatus such as a rickety chair or stool for doing an odd job.

The best way to avoid a fall is to become aware of the small dangers and avoid them. Fix frayed rugs, mend loose linoleum, keep a small secure stepladder handy for jobs that require climbing. If you do fall, relax your body and roll. Try not to stiffen or catch yourself on precarious objects that are in range.

☐ Choking

Choking occurs when a piece of food or other foreign body becomes lodged in the windpipe, making it impossible for the victim to breathe. A choking victim in extreme danger cannot speak or breathe, begins quickly to turn blue, and will often put his hand to his throat to indicate emergency. Action must be taken immediately to help someone who is choking. A choking victim can die in less than five minutes!

The most effective first-aid action for choking is the *Heimlich maneuver*. You apply the Heimlich maneuver by exerting pressure on the victim's diaphragm, which, in turn, compresses the air in the lungs and expels the food particle blocking the victim's breathing passage. (See the diagrams for complete instructions.) A choking victim can perform the Heimlich maneuver on himself if no help is at hand. He merely presses his own fist upward into his abdomen as described in method 1.

A victim of choking should be checked by a physician after the maneuver has been performed because injuries, such as severe bruising or even broken ribs, can result. Nevertheless, these injuries are minor compared with the lifesaving benefits of the Heimlich maneuver.

☐ Heimlich maneuver

Method 1: Victim standing or sitting, rescuer standing

1 The rescuer stands directly behind the victim and wraps his arms around the victim's waist.

2 The rescuer makes a fist with one hand and places his fist, thumb side against the victim's abdomen, between the victim's navel and rib cage.

3 The rescuer grasps his fist with his other hand and, with a sharp upward thrust, presses into the victim's abdomen.

4 The rescuer should repeat the maneuver several times until the victim stops choking.

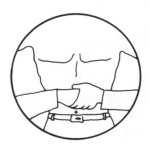

Method 2: Victim lying face up, rescuer kneeling

1 The rescuer should position the victim on his back.

2 The rescuer kneels facing the victim and straddling him with one knee on either side of the victim's hips.

3 With one hand on top of the other, the rescuer places the heel of the bottom hand on the victim's abdomen, slightly above the navel and below the rib cage.

4 With a sharp upward thrust, the rescuer presses his hand into the victim's abdomen.

5 The rescuer should repeat the maneuver several times until the victim stops choking.

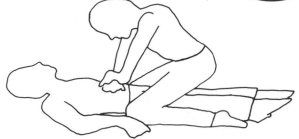

☐ Poisoning

Poisons can be found throughout the house: in medicine cabinets, under sinks, in the laundry room, basement, and garage. Most of us recognize the common poisons quickly and easily: cleaning liquids, ammonia, drugs, gasoline, paint thinner, and the like. However, often we neglect to note that such innocent and ubiquitous household items as aspirin, shampoo, cosmetics, mothballs (these can be especially dangerous because they look like candy), and laundry detergents can be lethal, especially if swallowed by a child.

Children are the most common victims of household poisoning. Hundreds of children die each year from accidental poisoning, and in most cases these tragedies could have been avoided.

Keep potent medicines and poisonous household liquids (cleaning liquids, paints, and cosmetics) locked up or, at least, out of reach of children. Warn older children of the dangers associated with these substances and instruct them in basic first-aid procedures.

If an accidental poisoning does occur, first and foremost, *remain calm.* Do the following in rapid sequence: find the container of the poisonous substance; *if you know which one to give*, administer the proper antidote; telephone your doctor, the emergency room of the nearest hospital, or your local poison-control center; tell your phone contact the name of the substance swallowed and read him the instructions for antidote given on the label; follow the phone contact's instructions; take the victim to an emergency room or doctor's office and be sure to *take the poison container with you.*

If you are not sure which antidote to administer, telephone your doctor, the emergency room of the nearest hospital, or your local poison-control center, and read them the label; follow the instructions given you for an antidote.

A note about syrup of ipecac: this nonprescription drug can be a lifesaver, especially for a child who is accidentally poisoned. By inducing vomiting, ipecac begins to clear the victim's body of the poisonous substance. Ipecac should *not* be given to a semiconscious or unconscious person, nor should it be used if the poison was lye, acid, or a petroleum product such as gasoline or paint thinner. In addition, ipecac should *not* be given together with milk or a carbonated beverage. After administering ipecac, take the victim immediately to the nearest emergency room or poison-control center.

Finally, become familiar with your local poison-control center; every city has at least one. Have the telephone number and address of the center nearest your home at your fingertips. Call the center when you even suspect someone has been poisoned.

☐ Common household poisons

MEDICINAL ITEMS

Antiseptics
Aspirin
Boric acid
Cough syrups
Iodine
Laxatives
Prescription medications
Rubbing alcohol, liniments
Vitamins

KITCHEN, LAUNDRY, AND CLEANING AIDS

Aerosols
Ammonia
Bleaches
Detergents
Drain cleaners
Dry-cleaning fluid
Dyes
Floor and rug cleaners
Furniture waxes and polishes
Lye
Metal and jewelry cleaners
Toilet-bowl cleaner

COSMETICS

Astringents
Colognes, perfumes
Cuticle remover, nail polish, polish remover
Depilatories (hair removers)
Hair lotions, creams, shampoos
Permanent-wave solutions
Shaving creams, lotions
Suntan creams, oils

GARAGE AND WORKSHOP ITEMS

Auto polishes, waxes
Gasoline
Insecticide sprays
Paints, varnishes, shellacs
Paint thinners, removers
Plastic mender, glues
Rat poison

MISCELLANEOUS HOUSEHOLD POISONS

Benzene
Deodorizers
Kerosene
Leather preservatives
Mothballs, moth crystals
Typewriter cleaner

☐ Electric shock

Electric shock is a common and serious household danger. Severe shock causes serious burns and can halt a victim's heart and respiration, which in turn can lead to death.

To avoid electric shock in your home, take note of all your electrical appliances and equipment. Make sure appliances such as toasters, blenders, radios, and lighting fixtures are in good repair. Check cords frequently and repair frayed cord immediately. Never use an appliance while you stand on a wet floor or when your hands are damp. In the bathroom, use electrical fixtures and appliances such as razors only with the utmost care. Never keep a radio or a table lamp in a bathroom.

If someone in your home does receive a serious electric shock, proceed as follows:

1 Check to see if the victim is in contact with a live wire. If he is, shut off the main current or pull the wire from the victim. Never use your bare hands or a damp or metallic object to pull a live wire. Water and metal conduct electricity, and you too will be shocked. Instead, use a dry stick, heavy rubber gloves, a dry cloth, or a newspaper to separate the victim from the wire.

2 Give artificial respiration (page 9) immediately.

3 Call for an ambulance and rush the victim to the hospital.

Electric shock can kill instantly. Take great pains to avoid electrical hazards in your home, and if someone does experience electric shock, be prepared to act with speed.

☐ Fire

Statistics surrounding the dangers of household fires are stunning: fire strikes 1,500 homes each day in the United States; among persons killed by fire, four out of five are victims of home fires; for every death by fire in the home, 100 people are seriously injured. Clearly, fire is the most dangerous and most damaging household hazard—to human life and health as well as to property.

Most household fires result from faulty electrical wiring and heating in the home, negligence while cooking, or carelessness while smoking. Have the wiring in your home checked every year or two; if you find fuses blowing or an outlet that seems to be faulty, call an electrician immediately. If you notice anything unusual about your heating, have your heating equipment serviced quickly. Take great care in the kitchen (see Chapter 2, "Safety in the Kitchen") as well.

Careless smoking habits may well be the chief cause of home fires. A lighted cigarette or cigar left unattended can cause a blaze in a matter of minutes; so can smoldering ashes in a wastebasket. Smoking in bed, of course, is extremely dangerous and should be taboo.

If fire breaks out in your house, the first rule is to get out as fast as you can. If you are caught in a smoky room, take short breaths, breathe through your nose, and crawl (air will be fresher close to the floor) to the point of escape. If you are caught in a room with a window, open the window at the top and bottom. Heat and smoke will go out the top, and you can breathe fresh air from the bottom. Before trying to escape through a door, feel it to see if it is hot. If it is, the door itself may be on fire or the fire may be worse in the next room. *Never open a hot door.* Use stairs, not an elevator, for escape; fire usually cuts the power that runs an elevator.

Once you have escaped, do not try to fight the fire yourself. Call the fire department, using the emergency telephone number or through an alarm box. Never go back into a burning building. Above all, attempt to remain calm. Escaping a fire requires ingenuity; panic caused by darkness, smoke, and heat can leave you paralyzed.

To prepare for a possible fire, keep fire extinguishers in your home. There are three basic types of extinguishers:

- Class A—use to extinguish fires of solid combustible materials such as wood, paper, and textiles.

- Class B—use to extinguish fires of flammable liquids and gases.

- Class C—use for electrical fires. This is a general-purpose extinguisher because it can put out fires of solids and gases.

Plan a fire-escape route. Practice using it and work out an alternate using various entrances to your house (see "A Family Fire Drill" opposite).

Consider installing one or more automatic smoke detectors. Smoke detectors sense smoke from a fire and then sound an alarm. Because smoke rises, the best place to install a detector is on the ceiling or high on an inside wall just below the ceiling. Halls, bedrooms, and at the tops and bottoms of stairwells are the best positions for smoke detectors.

Consider using flame-resistant fabrics in some areas of your home. Many kinds of fabrics are treated so that they are flame resistant; therefore, you can use this type of fabric in a variety of ways. While flame-resistant fabrics can burn, they resist being ignited and will usually stop burning as soon as the flame is removed.

Such fabric is especially recommended for the sleepwear of children, elderly people, and handicapped people—in other words, those who would have greater-than-normal difficulty escaping a fire. Children's Halloween costumes should also be made of flame-resistant materials. You might consider having curtains or upholstered furniture near a fireplace made of flame-resistant fabric. Most garments or fabrics treated with flame-resistant chemicals are so marked on their labels.

☐ A family fire drill

The following is a suggested procedure for a family fire drill. Make sure all members of your family participate in the drill and practice it every few months so that the procedure is crystal clear to each family member.

1   Draw a floor plan that includes every room in your house.

2   Plan an escape route from each room in the house. Study every possible escape route and select the quickest and the safest.

3   Plan an alternate escape route from each room in case one route is blocked by fire.

4   Avoid using interior stairwells and open halls for escape routes. Fire and smoke often collect in these areas.

5   Make sure that children can open all doors, windows, and screens in every escape route.

6   Assign specific responsibilities to every adult and older child. For example, Susan, age fourteen, is responsible for Bradley, age two. Father is responsible for Grandma.

7   Make sure that each family member knows the location of the fire-alarm box nearest to your home and knows how to set off the alarm.

8   Check bedroom doors carefully. Make sure each fits properly in its frame so that if fire breaks out, the door will serve well as a barricade.

9   Keep a flashlight handy in each bedroom to assist in a potential escape.

10   Select a meeting place outside the house for the family members to gather after they have escaped. This is the quickest way to determine if everyone has escaped. Try to select a lighted place, such as under a streetlight, in case fire strikes at night.

11   Impress on each family member the need to refrain from entering the burning building once he or she has escaped.

12   Impress on each member the importance of acting quickly and calmly.

☐ Firearms

More than 2,000 deaths occur each year as a result of improper use and storage of firearms. Most sportsmen are experts in the care and handling of their guns, but all family members, not just the hobbyist, should be fully aware of the danger and the use of firearms.

If a gun is in the house for protection, each adult should be instructed about how to use it safely. Guns should be locked up in a rack or cabinet and out of the reach of children.

☐ Children's toys

It is difficult to imagine that that adorable Teddy bear, that chunky wooden car, or that dimpled doll could potentially be a hazard to a child. However, each year 175,000 children are seriously cut, punctured, burned, or choked by seemingly harmless toys.

Before buying any toy for your children, ask yourself the following questions:

- Is this toy strongly constructed?
- Is it free of sharp edges or points?
- Is it free of tiny parts that can fall off and be swallowed?
- If it is a soft toy, is it flame resistant?
- If it has batteries or electrical attachments, are my children old enough to play with it safely and is the toy itself safe?

Read the labels on toys carefully. Often toy manufacturers will note that a specific toy is not appropriate for children under a certain age or that a certain game requires adult supervision. Teach your children to use toys safely and make sure the playthings are appropriate to your children's level of maturity.

Inspect your children's toys occasionally for signs of chipping or breaking. Make sure the button eyes on stuffed toys are sewn or glued securely in place and that wooden toys are free of splinters and rough edges.

Devise a special storage place for toys. A special toybox should have a lightweight lid that children can lift easily and safely and should be equipped with a device to hold the lid open securely. Teach your children to put their toys away when they're done playing. Neglected toys strewn around the house are a danger to all family members. Throw away dangerously damaged toys no matter how special they are to your children. Their safety is more important!

CHAPTER 2
Safety in the kitchen

The kitchen is one of the most often used rooms in the house. We prepare and often eat two or three meals there each day. We grab snacks, feed pets, wash dishes, polish silver, think about dieting, and, in general, live a large portion of our everyday lives in this one, very central room. Because so much is required of a kitchen (sufficient cooking equipment, ample storage areas, and adequate working space), it is a prime area for accidents.

☐ Safety with kitchen utensils

The modern kitchen, even the simplest one, contains equipment that if not used properly is potentially dangerous. Even the most elemental food-preparation tool, the knife, must be cleaned carefully and stored, if not in a special knife holder, then in a divided drawer and with the point away from the hand. (A knife should never be thrown loosely into a drawer where, unnoticed, its sharp edge can cause a serious cut.)

The two appliances we often take for granted, the refrigerator and the stove, can be dangerous if not checked regularly and used with care. It is easy to forget that a refrigerator is a very large, very powerful electrical appliance. It should be defrosted when ice collects to make sure that it cools food properly. To avoid electric shock, water should never be allowed to collect under the refrigerator. Children should be impressed with the fact that a refrigerator is not a toy. Tiny children are often fascinated with the idea of climbing into the refrigerator, but once in, are unable to get out. Each year many children suffocate in refrigerator accidents.

The stove, whether it is gas or electric, must be used with great care. A gas stove should be checked regularly to ensure that its pilot lights (both on the range and in the oven) are functioning properly. If you must use a match to ignite the burners, always light the match *before* turning on the gas. Better yet, if the pilot is not strong enough to ignite the burners without a match, have a repair person adjust the pilot light. Never work at a gas stove when you are wearing a flimsy or full garment. Floppy sleeves or a billowy nightgown can go up in flames instantly, causing serious burns.

(Text continues on page 24.)

Self-assessment

DO YOU:

	YES	NO
■ Avoid leaving opened jars or bottles that can spill in cabinets or in the refrigerator?	_____	_____
■ Use a sturdy, balanced stool or stepladder for climbing?	_____	_____
■ Avoid reaching for objects stored on shelves outside your line of vision?	_____	_____
■ Clean the broiler of the oven immediately after using it?	_____	_____
■ Always open a window or turn on a kitchen vent when cooking?	_____	_____
■ Light the match *before* turning on a gas burner or oven?	_____	_____
■ Dry your hands before operating an electrical appliance?	_____	_____
■ Avoid wearing loose, flimsy garments around the flame on a gas range?	_____	_____
■ Shield yourself from hot steam by always lifting the far side of a pan lid to check simmering food?	_____	_____
■ Use well-padded pot holders (not apron corners, dishtowels, or cloths) when handling hot pans?	_____	_____
■ Watch simmering pots carefully so that liquids do not boil over?	_____	_____
■ Avoid touching a warm burner on an electric range?	_____	_____
■ Refrigerate foods properly to prevent food poisoning?	_____	_____
■ Clean the kitchen floor regularly to avoid accidents resulting from grease spots, dirt, or water?	_____	_____
■ Store knives in a safety holder or, at least, with points directed away from the hand?	_____	_____

	YES	NO

- Store detergents, laundry products, plumbing products, and other poisonous substances out of the reach of children? _____ _____

- Store flammable chemical products away from sources of heat? _____ _____

- Make sure all potentially poisonous products (laundry detergents, plumbing and drain-cleaning liquids, cleaning fluids, etc.) are stored in their original containers with labels clearly visible? _____ _____

- Round the corners of cabinets, counters, tables, and hard chairs to prevent accidents? _____ _____

- Make a habit of closing cupboards, cabinets, and drawers? _____ _____

- Avoid hanging curtains near the range or other source of flame or heat? _____ _____

- Disconnect electrical appliances (except freezer, stove, and refrigerator) when you are not using them? _____ _____

- Replace cracked appliances or frayed cords immediately? _____ _____

- Make sure your kitchen is adequately wired to carry the amount of wattage your appliances require? _____ _____

- Check stove burners and pilot lights frequently to see that they burn evenly and no gas is leaking? _____ _____

- Store "attractive" foods (cookies, candies, etc.) in a spot where children can reach them safely? (Or else store them so it is *impossible* for children to find them?) _____ _____

- Turn pots and saucepans so their handles don't project over the edge of the stove? _____ _____

An electric stove poses different safety problems, but they can be equally serious. Often a burner that is not red may nevertheless be very hot. Never put your hand directly on a burner. Check the safety lights on your stove frequently. Like the refrigerator, the electric stove is a very powerful appliance. Have the wiring checked immediately if you suspect a problem.

Most of us have a number of smaller electrical appliances in our kitchens: blenders, food processors, toasters, can openers, garbage-disposal units, knife sharpeners—to name a few. Be sure each appliance is in top working condition; if it isn't, have it repaired. Check the cord each time you use an appliance to make sure it is not frayed or cracked.

Simple, old-fashioned pots and pans can be dangerous if not used properly. Check your utensils to be sure handles are tight and secure. If the handle breaks as you pick up a pot of boiling water, you could be badly burned. When you buy pots and pans, check labels carefully; some enameled and ceramic pots, if cracked, can poison food cooked in them. Finally, throw away worn, broken, and badly burned pans. They might break in use and cause a serious burn.

Every kitchen is stocked with cleaning equipment. Detergents, cleansers, ammonia products, and the like are all poisonous. Keep them out of the reach of children, and store them away from food and fire.

☐ Safe behavior in the kitchen

The kitchen is a *work*room, not a *play*room. Impress upon children that it is unsafe to run, jump, and slide in the kitchen. Teach them about various utensils, and be sure they know how to use each item correctly and safely before allowing them to "cook" alone. Don't allow the kitchen to become a running space for pets. They can easily get underfoot and cause accidents.

☐ Kitchen fires

More fires start in the kitchen than in any other part of the house. The reasons are obvious: the opportunities for foods to burn are many; the chance that an electrical fire will result from faulty wiring or equipment is high. It is easy to become careless while working in the kitchen; as a result, it is equally easy for fires to start.

Each kind of fire must be treated in a specific way.

- *Grease fire.* If the fire starts on the top of the stove, smother the flames with plain baking soda. Cover the pan or burning area with an iron lid. If a grease fire starts in the oven or broiler, close the oven door and turn off the heat. A grease fire must be smothered. Do not pour water on the flames. The excess liquid will only spread the fire.

■ *Electrical fire*. Unplug the appliance or shut off the electricity. Pour water onto the flames, but only *after* the electrical current has been shut off.

■ *Coal or wood fire*. Pour water directly over the flames.

■ *Kerosene or gasoline fire*. If the fire is small, smother with a pan lid. Like grease fires, a gasoline fire must be smothered. Do not pour water on the flames.

Do not attempt to put out a kitchen fire if it is quickly clear that the fire is large. Get out of the house as fast as you can and call the fire department.

□ General cleanliness

For reasons of both safety and health, it is imperative to keep your kitchen as clean as possible. After each meal, clear away and wash dishes and put away food. Many foods, such as butter and mayonnaise, will spoil unless kept refrigerated and should be put away after each meal. Wipe up spills as soon as they happen. Water or oily substances on a floor can cause skids and falls that may result in serious injury. If dishes and pots are left on counters when not in use, a careless sweep of a hand can cause a glass to break, which may result in a cut. Clean up a broken plate or glass immediately. (Use a wet paper towel to pick up the pieces. Sweep up every splinter.)

The kitchen should be well lighted so that anyone working or eating in the kitchen can see clearly. An overhead light is necessary in every kitchen. You might also consider having a lamp on a counter if there is space.

CHAPTER 3
Safety in the bathroom

Second only to the kitchen, the bathroom is potentially the most dangerous room in the house. About 180,000 injuries occur there every year as a result of falls, burns, electrocutions, and drownings. In addition, medicines and cosmetics, which can be poisonous if not used with caution, are often stored in the bathroom. Finally, the implements we usually use in the bathroom—razors being the primary culprits—can cause serious cuts.

Most of the surfaces in a bathroom—the tile floor and walls; the porcelain tub, sink, and toilet—become extremely slippery when wet. And, of course, they are often wet. To avoid *slips and falls*, use protective mats and handbars wherever possible. In the shower and tub, install a suction-rubber mat or adhesive appliqués to secure your footing. Place a rubber-backed rug on the floor and use a similar cloth cover on the toilet seat. Install handbars in the tub and shower; if the bathroom is used by children, an elderly person, or a handicapped person, put a handbar next to the toilet.

Never store glass bottles next to the tub; buy such products as shampoo and oils in plastic containers. If you wish a shower stall instead of a shower curtain, make sure it is made of safety glass or heavy-duty plastic.

Scalding water can cause serious *burns*. Always test the water before hopping into a tub or shower. Make sure your water heater has a temperature-control device so that you are not suddenly burned while in the shower.

Electrocutions frequently occur in the bathroom and are usually the result of carelessness. Never plug a radio, razor, hairdryer, or other appliance in a place where it could easily fall into a tub or sink. Never touch any electrical fixture or appliance with wet hands, while standing on a damp floor, or while you are in the tub or shower. When you disconnect an appliance, remove the cord from the wall outlet, not from the appliance itself. Never leave a cord or appliance dangling from a wall outlet; it can literally kill if it is dropped or knocked into a sink filled with water.

A child, an elderly person, or a handicapped person can easily *drown* in a bathtub. Never leave a child unattended in the bathroom, particularly while he is bathing, and keep a watchful eye on the elderly or handicapped. Be alert to an unusually long stay in the bathtub; check if you become suspicious—do not allow the bathroom door to be locked.

Self-assessment

DO YOU:

	YES	NO
■ Check the temperature of bath or shower water with your hand before bathing to prevent scalding?	_____	_____
■ Avoid leaving an infant alone in the bathtub?	_____	_____
■ Avoid storing glass bottles or jars near the bathtub?	_____	_____
■ Leave a window or door open slightly while bathing to prevent steam condensation from making the floor slippery?	_____	_____
■ Avoid using electrical appliances near the bathtub?	_____	_____
■ Avoid taking medicine in the dark or without reading the label carefully?	_____	_____
■ Discard prescription medicine when the illness for which it is prescribed is over?	_____	_____
■ Keep all medicines out of the reach of children?	_____	_____
■ Mark all medicines carefully and heed such directions as ''for external use only''?	_____	_____
■ Discard razor blades by wrapping them carefully or dropping them into a safety disposal slot?	_____	_____
■ Have your shower or tub enclosure constructed of safety glass or plastic?	_____	_____
■ Always dry the bathroom floor after a shower or bath?	_____	_____
■ Provide nonskid appliqués or rubber mats for the bathtub and shower?	_____	_____
■ Provide nonskid rugs for the bathroom floor?	_____	_____
■ Provide adequate soap dishes to prevent soap from sliding into the tub or shower or onto the floor?	_____	_____
■ Install handbars in the tub, shower, and near the toilet?	_____	_____
■ Install clothes hooks above eye level to prevent face and eye injuries?	_____	_____
■ Equip your automatic water heater with a temperature control to avoid scalding water?	_____	_____

CHAPTER 4
Safety in the basement, workshop, and garage

In many houses, the basement, workshop, garage, and storage areas become dumping grounds for all those cumbersome or infrequently used goods we hate to throw away: suitcases, Christmas decorations, tools, broken toys, magazines, newspapers, baby clothes, furniture—the list is nearly endless. As a result, these spaces often become littered and messy, and if highly combustible materials are stored there, fire can easily result.

As a general rule, keep these rooms as orderly as possible. Weed out magazines and papers, old clothing, and general unused litter at regular intervals. Don't allow a mess to accumulate. Store the items you wish to keep in boxes, chests, and storage cabinets. Label the containers and put them in a place where they will remain clean, dry, and out of the way. Install secure hooks and holders on the walls and put things away in an orderly manner.

☐ Safety in the basement

In some homes the basement is the laundry room and the weekend workshop as well as a storage space. It is also where the water heater, gas or oil burner, and the central electrical service panel are located.

Make sure you understand how your water heater, gas or oil burner, and electrical panel operate. If their operation is unclear to you, have a plumber and an electrician explain it to you. Ask yourself or your electrician if the electrical service panel has enough capacity for the needs of your house. You should be using 15-ampere fuses; the presence of 20- or 30-ampere fuses indicates that you have too few circuits and the wiring is overloaded. If fuses blow frequently, find the cause and remedy it; don't just replace the blown fuse with one of higher amperage. Overloaded circuits cause fires.

Keep your *laundry area* clean and workable. Wipe off the washer and dryer occasionally and check to see that the electrical circuits or gas units are strong enough to support them. (Have them checked by your gas company representative or an electrician if you are in doubt.) Try to make space to install a table on which to fold clothes and store supplies. Never string a clothesline in a low-ceilinged basement; use a standing rack.

Self-assessment

DO YOU:

	YES	NO
■ Keep small items, such as nails, screws, and tiny tools, in boxes or jars rather than lying loose?	_____	_____
■ Keep all tools, especially power tools, out of the reach of children?	_____	_____
■ Keep work areas well ventilated and well lighted?	_____	_____
■ Have a first-aid kit close at hand?	_____	_____
■ Wear protective clothing, such as safety glasses or earplugs, while working on jobs that require such measures?	_____	_____
■ Destroy oil-soaked rags immediately and avoid storing them?	_____	_____
■ Call the gas company or plumber immediately if you suspect a leaky valve or pipe?	_____	_____
■ Keep your garage, basement, and workshop neat and orderly at all times?	_____	_____
■ Always open the garage door before running the car engine inside?	_____	_____
■ Check the area around the car before backing out?	_____	_____
■ Use a cart to move heavy trash, garbage, or equipment?	_____	_____
■ Know how to change a fuse and always have spare fuses on hand?	_____	_____
■ Always turn off the main switch before changing a fuse?	_____	_____
■ Label all fuses and circuit breakers to identify outlets and fixtures they protect?	_____	_____
■ Know where your main gas and water valves are located and how to turn them off?	_____	_____

Self-assessment
(continued)

DO YOU:

	YES	NO
■ Know where your main electric switch is located and how to turn it off?	_____	_____
■ Know the proper fuse ratings for the electrical circuits in your house and garage?	_____	_____
■ Know how to light the pilot light on your furnace and water heater?	_____	_____
■ Store flammable liquids (such as kerosene, paint thinner, and turpentine) in safety containers and away from heat sources?	_____	_____
■ Have your furnace, chimney, and flues inspected and cleaned once a year by professionals?	_____	_____
■ Inspect lift-up garage doors regularly for safe operation?	_____	_____
■ Keep power tools properly grounded?	_____	_____
■ Keep power-tool guards in place?	_____	_____

☐ Safety in the workshop

In most home workshops, paints, thinners, and other *flammable liquids* are commonplace. Be careful how you use and store them. Never use flammable liquid around a flame—including a match, cigarette, pilot light, furnace, and heater. Always use it outdoors or in a well-ventilated area to avoid vapor poisoning. Never fill the tank of any gasoline-powered equipment, such as a lawn mower, when the engine is running or still hot; shut the engine off and allow it to cool before refueling. To siphon gasoline, use a hand pump; never put gasoline near your mouth. Finally, never store gasoline in the trunk of your car or strapped to the outside. The vapors can ignite and cause an explosion.

Keep flammable liquids in safety cans that have flame arresters and pressure-release valves; store the containers away from your house. Try to buy minimum quantities of any flammable liquids. Label their containers clearly and keep them out of the reach of children.

If a flammable liquid does catch fire, extinguish the blaze with a carbon dioxide or dry chemical fire extinguisher. (Keep an extinguisher near your work space.) Never use water.

When using *power tools*, be sure to read all operating, maintenance, and safety instructions carefully. The following are a few general tips for using power tools safely:

- Select the proper tool for the job.

- Keep guards in place and in good working order.

- Dress safely for the job. Wear sturdy shoes. Wear safety glasses to protect your eyes. Do not wear loose clothing or jewelry that may catch in moving parts.

- Do not overreach. Maintain good footing and balance.

- Do not work when you are tired, rushed, or anxious. This can lead to accidents.

- Keep the work area free of clutter. Move cables and cords out of the way.

- Wait until the motor is off and the tool unplugged before repairing or cleaning it.

- Make sure the tool is turned off and unplugged when not in use.

- Keep children away from the work area. Never allow them to operate tools.

- Use a vise or clamp, when appropriate, to hold work in place.

- Always use a tool equipped with double insulation or a grounded plug.

- Do not operate an electrical tool in a damp area.

- If a tool runs very hot, have it tested immediately (and repaired).

- Avoid using an extension cord. If you must use one, make sure it is of a suitable weight and of the same ampere rating as the tool.

- Never use a metal ladder when making electrical repairs. The metal conducts electricity.

- Keep tools and cords away from heat, oil, and sharp edges.

- Disconnect a tool by holding the plug, not by pulling on the cord.

- Repair any damaged tool immediately. Check the cable for breaks, loose connections, and bare wires. Check the prongs for security.

☐ Safety in the garage

The garage often does multiple duty as garden shed, workshop, and general storage space in addition to being the home for your automobile. It is important to make a habit of keeping the garage free of clutter. Securely hang as much equipment as possible (with the heaviest portion down); store other tools and supplies in containers. Tidy up after each work session in the garage.

Garage doors can cause injuries. The safety mechanisms of a powered door should be adjusted occasionally to make sure they run smoothly; a manually operated door should be opened and closed with care to prevent pinching (even breaking) a finger in the hinges. Keep the door closed and locked to deter children and trespassers from coming in.

Carbon monoxide poison is a common danger in garages because it is produced by the combustion of the gasoline when a car engine is running. Never start an auto engine in a closed garage. Not only can people in the car be killed, but those in an adjoining room may also be poisoned.

☐ A word about carbon monoxide

Other household appliances, such as gas heaters, may also produce carbon monoxide. Be sure to buy equipment that complies with national safety standards. (Check for a seal from the American Gas Association—AGA— or the Underwriters' Laboratories—UL.) Have a qualified serviceperson install and inspect any fuel-burning appliance. A heater should be vented to the outside with flue pipes that are fitted correctly and in good repair. Finally, never burn charcoal, which can release dangerous amounts of carbon monoxide, in an enclosed or unventilated area.

Carbon monoxide is colorless, odorless, tasteless, and lethal. Learn which of your household appliances can produce carbon monoxide and use them with great caution.

CHAPTER 5
Safety outdoors and in the yard

Good safety habits are just as important outside as they are inside. A family spends a great amount of time outdoors—repairing the house, working in the garden, mowing the lawn, shoveling snow, playing with the children, cooking out. All these activities, enjoyable as some are, can be dangerous, and it is important to be aware of hazards and to avoid them.

When cleaning windows or painting the outside of the house, use the sturdiest ladder available. Never stand on the top rung. Keep your weight centered; don't twist or bend or reach too far for any reason—this throws you off balance.

Be aware of potential hazards on the grounds of your property. A dip in the ground, a small hill, or a hole dug for a cistern can be dangerous to running children or to anyone strolling across the lawn. Draw attention to the hazard with a fence, shrubbery, or a flower bed to prevent people from tripping or falling.

Check your driveway and sidewalks. If the surfaces are too smooth, they can be extremely slippery when wet. Beware! If the surfaces are broken or cracked, have them repaired immediately.

Self-assessment

DO YOU:

	YES	NO
■ Exercise great care when using a ladder to put up screens, to paint, or to repair the outside of the house?	_____	_____
■ Keep ladders in excellent repair by replacing loose rungs and, on extension ladders, frayed ropes?	_____	_____
■ Avoid working on a ladder in windy weather?	_____	_____
■ Keep children and pets at a safe distance when operating your power mower?	_____	_____
■ Shut off a power mower when cleaning it or emptying the grass catcher?	_____	_____
■ Never refuel a power mower when the motor is running or warm?	_____	_____
■ Avoid overexerting yourself shoveling snow?	_____	_____
■ Secure a helper for heavy outdoor work if the job seems strenuous?	_____	_____
■ Use caution when starting a charcoal fire?	_____	_____
■ Never leave a barbecue burning without making sure someone is watching the fire?	_____	_____
■ Use heat-resistant mitts and long-handled utensils for cookouts?	_____	_____

	YES	NO
■ Keep the yard clear of broken glass, nail-studded boards, and other litter that could cause injuries?	_____	_____
■ Cover all holes such as those for cisterns or drains?	_____	_____
■ Keep fences in good repair and secure?	_____	_____
■ String clotheslines above head height?	_____	_____
■ Keep steps and sidewalks clear of tools, toys, ice, and snow?	_____	_____
■ Return garden tools to their storage place after use?	_____	_____
■ Repair broken walks and driveways promptly?	_____	_____
■ Know how to install properly and maintain outdoor play equipment?	_____	_____
■ Provide a safe play area for your children?	_____	_____
■ Check children's play equipment frequently to make sure it is secure and in good repair?	_____	_____
■ Instruct children in safe play habits around outdoor play equipment?	_____	_____
■ Always supervise children when they are playing in a pool?	_____	_____

☐ Cooking outdoors

Cooking outdoors presents the same hazards as cooking in the kitchen—and then some! Observe the same rules you would in the kitchen about lifting hot and heavy pans and working with fire. In addition, follow these rules:

- Start a charcoal fire only with fuel specifically labeled as a charcoal starter. Never use gasoline.

- Do not add fuel to the fire after it is lit. The flames could travel up the can and cause an explosion or ignite your clothing.

- Instruct children to stay clear of the fire. (Because cooking out is usually special, children are often fascinated. Watch them carefully.)

- Never burn charcoal in an enclosed area. Dangerous amounts of carbon monoxide can be released.

- Allow the charcoal to burn out in a safe place. Use a movable charcoal grill.

Cooking out is usually considered a leisure-time, fun activity. As a result, defenses and awareness are often dulled. Be extra careful.

☐ Playground equipment

Playground equipment—swings, slides, seesaws, and monkey bars—can provide an opportunity for your children to exercise, learn, and generally have fun. However, use of these toys often results in accidents if the equipment itself is unsafe or if children are not instructed how to use it properly.

Select the equipment you buy with great care. Install it according to instructions; if you are in doubt, ask someone who is an expert to help you. Put swings and slides at least 6 feet from fences, buildings, walls, and walkways, as well as from other play spaces, such as sandboxes. Set the legs of a gym set in concrete and then place the concrete underground to prevent tripping. Be sure the equipment is on the grass or on soft ground such as sand. Never install equipment on concrete, blacktop, brick, or cinder.

Check the equipment routinely. Tighten any loose nuts, bolts, or hooks. Apply tape over protruding screws or other sharp edges. Replace worn parts, such as rusted swing chains or worn ropes on climbing nets or tire swings. Sand and repaint (with unleaded paint) rusted metal. Keep landing pits clear of debris and refill them with sand at regular intervals.

☐ Instructing children at play

Kids are pretty smart. They can learn rules—and follow them. But first they have to be told. The following are a few rules to teach children to practice when using playground equipment.

SWINGS

- Have only one person in a swing at a time.
- Hold on with both hands.
- Sit in the center of the swing.
- Never stand or kneel in a swing.
- Never swing empty seats or twist swing chains.
- Stay away from the back or front of a moving swing.

SLIDES

- Use the steps to the slide.
- Never climb up the sliding surface.
- Be sure everyone is out of the way before sliding down.
- Slide down one at a time, feet first.
- Always sit up.

SEESAWS

- Sit forward on a seesaw, partners facing one another.
- Hold on with both hands.
- Be sure each partner has both feet on the ground before starting.

CLIMBING EQUIPMENT

- Climb only on equipment made for climbing.
- Hold on tightly when climbing.
- Avoid bumping or stepping on others.

CHAPTER 6
Crime prevention around the house

Protecting your house from possible burglary is one of the most important aspects of household safety. Many crimes—robberies, burglaries, vandalism, rape, even murder—happen at random; criminals are disturbed people, and some will strike merely because they have the opportunity. It is your responsibility to minimize the temptation as much as you possibly can.

☐ General protective measures

The more difficult it is to enter a house, the less attractive the attempt will seem to an intruder. An unlocked door, an open garage, a dark house, an open window are all invitations to a potential criminal. Keep doors locked even if you are at home. You could be in the backyard pulling weeds while a burglar quietly walks off with your television set! Many professional thieves scour newspapers for notices of weddings and anniversaries and then rob a house (all those presents!) while the happy couple—and all other family members—are partying. It's best not to publicize such events in advance; if you do, refrain from printing the time of day of the celebration. Better yet, hire a guard during the hours you'll be away from the house on such an occasion.

When you go out in the evening—or any other time of day, for that matter—create the illusion that the house is occupied. Most criminals are reluctant to enter a house when they believe people are present. Leave several *lights* on in the house. Install outside lights at each doorway and near the garage and leave them on whether you are at home or away. Leave lights on in the kitchen, living room, and a bedroom when you go out. A single light will not fool even a novice thief; without being excessive, light those areas you might be using were you at home.

A *radio* uses little electricity and gives the impression that someone is home. Install a radio near a doorway and turn it on as you leave. A *dog* is also helpful in deterring robbers. Even a tiny dog will create enough commotion to scare off a would-be criminal. Adjust *window shades* or *blinds* the way you would if you were home. A home with all shades drawn, particularly in daylight hours, strongly hints that the occupants are away.

Not only that, drawn shades can actually protect the thief as he rummages through your house!

An *alarm system* can also be useful. There are two kinds of systems: an alarm that sounds only on the premises, which might scare the burglar (but might also go unheard by a neighbor), and a central system that sounds at a local police station. An alarm system can be annoying because it can be triggered easily by a family member instead of a burglar. Before installing a system, seek advice from a professional about the most hassle-free system. Your police department may have a list of approved devices.

Another way to protect your house from burglary is to join the *Operation Identification Program*. With the program, you code each valuable piece with a number (which is etched onto appliances and other valuables) and register the number with the police department. You then put a sticker on your door or window advertising your association with the program. Statistics show that burglars are then aware that they will have trouble disposing of stolen goods and are reluctant to enter. If you are robbed, your chance of reclaiming your possessions is greater if they have been registered with Operation Identification.

☐ Protective measures for apartment dwellers

Apartment dwellers must exercise the same protective measures as those who live in houses, but they have additional problems. Common areas in the apartment building—hallways, stairwells, elevators, laundry and storage rooms, and the main doorway—must also be protected.

It is a good idea to get together with neighbors and take steps to make sure your building is properly protected. To limit access to the building, install a buzzer-intercom system that connects the main door with each apartment. Never allow a stranger to enter the building, and make sure all tenants follow this rule religiously. If you have a doorman or guard, instruct him to announce each visitor.

For information about forming a block association or a tenants' security group, contact the crime-prevention officer at your local police station.

Self-assessment

DO YOU:

	YES	NO
■ Avoid publicizing, directly or indirectly, your vacation plans or special family social functions, such as weddings or anniversaries? (Professional burglars watch for such events.)	___	___
■ Suspend mail services or arrange to have mail forwarded while you are on vacation?	___	___
■ Halt all delivery services, such as milk delivery, with instructions to resume service only on your personal order?	___	___
■ Transfer valuables to a bank deposit box, especially if you will be away for several weeks?	___	___
■ Make arrangements for regular lawn care if you are planning to be away for several weeks?	___	___
■ Notify a close friend or relative of your vacation plans and ask him or her to keep an eye on the house for you?	___	___
■ Keep your garage door locked at all times?	___	___
■ Avoid leaving notes on the door telling a friend or relative where you have gone and when you will return?	___	___
■ Always leave some lights on when you leave the house in the evening?	___	___
■ Leave a radio on when you leave the house?	___	___
■ Always lock the windows before you go out?	___	___
■ Avoid leaving a key under the doormat or hidden anywhere else outside the house?	___	___
■ Avoid telling strangers when you will be away?	___	___
■ Check that all doors with hinges exposed on the outside have nonremovable hinge pins?	___	___
■ Repair weak or loose-fitting door frames promptly?	___	___
■ Report suspicious-looking strangers or unidentified parked cars in the neighborhood to the police emergency number?	___	___

	YES	NO
■ Check that spring locks are not used on any outside doors?	_____	_____
■ Check that all accessible windows have secure locking mechanisms?	_____	_____
■ Arrange to have Social Security or pension checks deposited directly into your bank account so that they never are loose in your mailbox?	_____	_____
■ Have the outside doors of your house constructed of solid-core wood, $1^3/_4$ inches thick?	_____	_____
■ Make sure doors fit snugly in their frames?	_____	_____
■ Make sure sliding glass doors are constructed of high-security plastic or safety glass?	_____	_____
■ Make sure sliding glass doors are secured by an additional means other than just a latch?	_____	_____
■ Make sure outside doors are equipped with either drop-bolt or dead-bolt locks?	_____	_____
■ Make sure each outside door is equipped with a window or peephole and a chain lock?	_____	_____
■ Know about the Federal Crime Insurance Program?	_____	_____
■ Know about homeowner's insurance policies?	_____	_____
■ Know about Operation Identification?	_____	_____

IF YOU LIVE IN AN APARTMENT BUILDING, IS:

■ A sturdy lock installed on the front door of the apartment building?	_____	_____
■ The outside door kept locked at all times?	_____	_____
■ The front door one that automatically closes and locks after being opened?	_____	_____
■ A buzzer system connected to the front door?	_____	_____

☐ Secure doors

To protect your home against burglary, start with your outside doors. Most intruders will try to get through a door before resorting to more complex measures; therefore, a secure door is the first and best source of protection.

Regardless of the strength of your door, if it fits loosely in the frame, it can be pried open. Strengthen a weak or loose-fitting door frame by putting wood spacers between the frame and the door. If you have a metal door frame installed in a masonry wall, fill the space with mortar.

A door with glass panels is easily broken by a burglar. Strengthen the door by backing the glass with metal sheeting, a protective mesh grill, laminated glass, or an acrylic plastic. These are all strong deterrents. You may wish to replace the door altogether with a solid-core wooden door, at least $1^3/_4$ inches thick. This is the safest door of all, although it is expensive.

Check that the mail slot is not within reach of the inside doorknob or lock. It is an easy trick for a burglar to open a lock by slipping his hand or a wire through a mail slot.

A *sliding glass door* is particularly vulnerable. The door can be easily removed by lifting it off the groove. To prevent this, install spacers or protruding screw heads in the groove. A weak latch can be easily broken by prying the door away from the frame. Place a piece of pipe or broom handle in the bottom groove. This secures the door if the latch is broken. Finally, add a stronger lock if the original lock is weak. Special sliding-door locks are available; some are designed especially to prevent removal of the door itself.

☐ Secure locks

Every outside door should be equipped with either a drop-bolt lock or a dead-bolt lock. Do not rely on a spring lock, which works simply by closing the door. It can be easily opened with a plastic card or other slip device. A drop-bolt or dead-bolt lock can be locked only with a key. A drop bolt should extend at least 1 inch into its receptacle to prevent the lock from being forced. A vertical bolt (another type of dead bolt) is particularly effective in resisting burglars.

A buttress-type lock (sometimes called a police lock) uses a long steel bar that fits into a floor receptacle and wedges against the inside of the door to prevent the door from being pried open. This type of lock is necessary if your door frame is weak and cannot be strengthened. Keep the bolt receptacle clean and free of small objects or other debris. The bolt will not engage fully if the hole is clogged.

Take great care when buying a lock and don't be afraid to splurge on the best lock you can get. Often what appears to be good brass is nothing more than brass-plated soft metal. Soft metal breaks easily and therefore offers little protection. Avoid inexpensive security products. The extra money you spend on the best equipment will be well worthwhile. Moreover, if you buy *one* very secure lock, you will have no need for extra locks. They add little security and can be a hazard in a fire or other emergency.

☐ Secure windows

Any window that can be reached from the street, a porch or terrace, a fire escape, or a roof needs extra security measures of some sort. Check each window to see that its lock is in good condition. The crescent-shaped locking device on most double-hung windows is rarely secure. It is easy to pry and dislodge.

For extra security, you can do several things:

- Drill a hole through both the lower-window and upper-window frames of double-hung windows. Insert a long nail into the hole. (Drill a second set of holes if you wish to have the window slightly ajar at times.)

- Use a key lock (either slide or barrel bolt) that locks both frames closed. This provides better protection because it prevents the window from being opened by a burglar who breaks a glass pane: he still needs a key to open the lock. For your own protection, do not use a key-lock device if the window must be used as a fire escape.

- Put special plastic or laminated glass into your windows. This can be expensive, but the windows cannot be broken.

- Install bars or gates with locks on vulnerable windows. For emergency-exit windows, accordion gates that can be opened from the inside, but not from the outside, are the best. (For safety in a fire, keep the key hidden but near the window.)

- For crank-type casement windows, remove the crank by unscrewing it from the handle. Store it in a place away from the window but near enough for your own use in case of emergency.

☐ Homeowner's insurance

A homeowner's insurance policy protects you against loss resulting from theft and fire. Check with your insurance agent or broker about a policy that is adequate for your needs. A simple policy may be sufficient, but if you have many valuables, you may require a personal property "floater" that costs somewhat more.

If you already have insurance, review it each year to make sure you are covered for at least 80 percent of the replacement value of your house and its contents. If you do not have insurance, check into acquiring some immediately. Even if you rent your home, you can get a policy designed for tenants.

☐ Federal crime insurance program

In 1971, the Federal Insurance Administration of the U.S. Department of Housing and Urban Development initiated a government program providing insurance policies to protect homeowners against burglary and robbery losses. Rates vary depending upon the crime rate of the individual community. To meet eligibility requirements, exterior doors and accessible windows in your home must meet standards specified by the program.

This program is available in Alabama, Arkansas, Colorado, Connecticut, Delaware, Florida, Georgia, Illinois, Iowa, Kansas, Maryland, Massachusetts, Minnesota, Missouri, New Jersey, New York, Ohio, Pennsylvania, Rhode Island, Tennessee, Virginia, and the District of Columbia.

Obtain an application for a Federal Crime Insurance policy from any licensed property-insurance agent or broker in the eligible states. Or you may write or call:

Federal Crime Insurance
P.O. Box 41033
Washington, D.C. 20014
800-638-8780 (toll free)

CHAPTER 7
Crime prevention for yourself

It is even more important to protect yourself against crime than it is to protect your home. Robbery, mugging, rape, and even murder are always possibilities, especially in big cities. But you can take precautions to make yourself as safe as possible.

☐ General safety tips

Be alert at all times when you are out. Look around you and be aware of who is standing near you or walking ahead of or behind you. *Be determined.* If you are on an unfamiliar or lonely street, quicken your pace and behave as though you were meeting someone. Always walk in well-lighted places. Stay away from dark buildings, doorways, alleys, walls, or high shrubbery. Know where you are walking. Try to stay on streets that are active and busy. Notify police immediately of suspicious-looking persons who are loitering, trying locked doors, or cruising in cars. Do not wait to be a victim.

If you are mugged or held up, do not resist. Give up your handbag, wallet, money, and do not try to attack the robber; he may do you harm. If you are the victim of a crime, report it to the police immediately. Take note of the sex, race, clothing, build, voice, and any peculiarities of the criminal and give the police as much detail as possible.

Self-assessment

DO YOU:

	YES	NO
■ Always use a peephole or chain lock so you can identify visitors before permitting them to enter your house?	_____	_____
■ Avoid allowing strangers to enter your house?	_____	_____
■ Make it a habit always to lock your door, even when you are at home?	_____	_____
■ Watch out for suspicious-looking people or cars in your neighborhood?	_____	_____
■ Leave a key to your house or apartment only with a trusted friend or relative?	_____	_____
■ Report to police any harassing calls you receive on the telephone?	_____	_____
■ Avoid giving your name, address, or telephone number to strangers?	_____	_____
■ Make an effort to become acquainted with your neighbors?	_____	_____
■ Make sure doorways (or, in apartment buildings, entrances and hallways) are well lighted?	_____	_____
■ Use only qualified and trustworthy household help, such as baby-sitters, cleaners, and companions?	_____	_____
■ Accept baby-sitting or other household jobs only from people you know or who have been recommended to you?	_____	_____

	YES	NO

- If you accept a job in another house, always give a relative or trusted friend the name, address, and telephone number of the person you are working for? _____ _____

- List only your last name and initials in the phone directory and on the mailbox, particularly if you are a woman living alone? _____ _____

- Avoid opening the door automatically after a knock? _____ _____

- Leave lights on near doors you will be using when you return home after dark? _____ _____

- Always have your key ready when you return home so you can open the door immediately? _____ _____

- Avoid entering your apartment or home if a window or door has been forced or broken? _____ _____

- Know what to do if you are mugged? _____ _____

- Know what to do if you are raped? _____ _____

- Know how to protect yourself from purse snatching? _____ _____

- Know what to do if you are awakened at night by an intruder? _____ _____

☐ Intruders in your home

If you return home and find your door is open or has been tampered with, do *not* enter the house or apartment. Go to a neighbor, call the police, and wait until the police arrive.

If you interrupt the burglar, remain as calm as possible. Do not antagonize him. Follow any instructions he gives; when he leaves, try to see which way he goes and note any distinguishing features. Call the police immediately.

If you awaken in the night and hear an intruder, stay in bed and pretend to be asleep. Call the police when the burglar leaves. If the intruder confronts you, give up money and possessions rather than risk violence or physical injury.

If you hear or see a prowler near your house, make noise and call the police. If someone is already attempting to break in, try to get out and call the police from a neighbor's telephone.

☐ Preventing mugging

To avoid the possibility of mugging, always appear determined and directed when you are walking on the street. Have your house key in your hand before you reach the door of your house, so that you can open your door quickly and safely. When you are out, do not exhibit large amounts of money; do not wear expensive jewelry or furs.

If you feel that someone is following you, go into a nearby store and call the police. If no telephone is handy, shout, scream, and call for help. Your noise will not only bring assistance, but should also scare off the would-be attacker.

At home, open your door only when you are certain of the caller's identity. Never open a door to a stranger.

☐ In case of rape

Despite precaution against crime, rape is an ever-present threat. If you are the victim of rape, do not be afraid or ashamed to tell authorities. Report the crime immediately to police. If you prefer to speak to a female officer, inform the policemen who respond at the scene and they will surely oblige.

Do not do anything to change your appearance before the police arrive. Do not douche or wash yourself or your clothing or alter anything else that may serve as evidence.

Have general medical and gynecological examinations as soon as possible, and try to have a police officer accompany you to the hospital or doctor's office. If your community has a rape crisis center, check into services available. Rape is a serious crime and should be treated as such.

☐ Reducing losses from purse snatching

When you leave the house, take only the money and credit cards you will need for that day. Divide valuables among your pockets, handbag, and wallet. You might even pin money to the inside of an article of clothing.

Keep your keys in a separate pocket. Keys found in your handbag combined with identification invite the purse snatcher to rob your house or apartment.

Carry a handbag with a short loop handle and hold it close to your body, tucked under your arm. Do not carry a bag that dangles from your shoulder. Never carry a handbag or a shopping bag looped around your wrist. If someone tries to snatch it from you, you could be injured.

In a theater or restaurant, keep your handbag on your lap. Do not place it on the floor, on another seat, or over the back of your chair. Never put your handbag down on a counter or in a shopping cart when you are in a store.

Never fight with a purse snatcher. You might be seriously injured in an attempt to save a few things that usually can be replaced.

☐ Safety hints for household help

If you agree to work in someone's home as a baby-sitter, helper, or other job, give the name, address, and telephone number of your employer to a family member or friend. Make clear arrangements for transportation to and from the job. If you are a teenage baby-sitter, ask for an escort. Do not accept a job if you do not know the employer or have some recommendation for him or her.

While working in another person's house, you should be responsible for several things. Guard against strangers. Check and lock doors and windows and do not unlock a door for anyone. Be suspicious about strange noises, a face at the window, or a worrisome phone call. If you are frightened, don't hesitate to call a neighbor or the police.

In case of fire, get children or other people you are caring for out of the house. Then call the fire department from a nearby telephone.

Guard against accidents. Pick up stray toys and be alert to possible household hazards. Do not operate an appliance unless you are familiar with it and have been told you may use it.

Make sure the employer informs you of his or her whereabouts and provides you with name, address, and telephone number where he or she can be reached. An employer should also supply the numbers of police, fire department, doctor, and a close relative so that you can summon help if an emergency arises.

☐ Safety tips for apartment dwellers

Most apartment dwellers are not well acquainted with other people in the building, but it is important to get to know your neighbors, at least casually. Use laundry and storage rooms only at appointed times and try never to be alone in them, particularly at night. Notify the management about any needed repairs, such as burnt-out lights or broken windows.

Get into the habit of using the door's peephole and chain lock. Always check who is knocking before opening the door, and *never* open the door to a stranger.

Be cautious when using the elevator. If you find yourself in the lobby with a stranger, let him take the elevator first; you wait for it to return. If you are in the elevator and someone gets in who seems suspicious, get off at the next floor. Always stand near the control panel. If you are attacked or held up, hit the alarm button and as many buttons as you can. This will allow the doors to open at several floors.

☐ Safety tips for women alone

If you are a woman living alone, list only your last name and initials in the telephone directory and on your mailbox. Keep your door locked at all times, even if you are at home. If you leave even for only a few minutes to walk the dog or collect the mail, get into the habit of locking the door.

Be cautious about unidentified telephone callers. If the caller does not identify himself, hang up. Do not get drawn into a conversation with an unknown caller. Moreover, never reveal your name, address, marital status, or any information indicating that you are alone.

Women alone are prime targets for thieves and rapists. Be very cautious.

☐ Special hints for the elderly

The elderly are easy targets for thieves and muggers. If you are an older person, especially if you live alone, you can take a number of measures to make your life safer.

Keep your door locked at all times. Always use the peephole to identify a caller, and never allow a stranger to enter your apartment. Exchange telephone numbers with neighbors living near you. Arrange a system of checking and group protection by using signals. Arrange to have your Social Security and other checks mailed directly to your bank.

Avoid entering your apartment building if you see a suspicious-looking person loitering in front, standing in the lobby, or riding in the elevator. Never use the laundry room if you are alone.

Travel and shop with friends or an escort as much as possible. Never carry a large sum of money or other valuables such as jewelry when you are out. Carry your keys in a pocket and have them ready when you enter the house.

If you are the victim of a crime, report the incident promptly to the police. If you are injured, you may be eligible for crime compensation if the crime is reported quickly. Ask your police department for an application form.

Contact a senior-citizen center, club, or social-service agency designated to give assistance to elderly victims of crime. Police can tell you how to go about obtaining replacements for stolen Medicare or other identification cards and can help you apply for emergency assistance, such as temporary housing, transportation service, or escort service for the elderly.

Several cities (Chicago, New York, New Orleans, Los Angeles, Washington, D.C., and Milwaukee) have special programs to provide crisis counseling, transportation, home care, medical aid, and other services for elderly victims of crime. In addition, they have safety programs to teach elderly people how to protect themselves from crime. If you live in or near one of these cities, contact your local police department for information about the programs.

☐ For victims of domestic violence

A network of support services now exists and is being further developed throughout the country. These are the options presently open:

1 If he/she is being hurt, threatened, or is in jeopardy—call the local police.

2 If he/she needs ongoing protection, the victim may go to family court or criminal court. No attorney is required.

3 Your county department of social services will provide emergency aid for shelter, plus ongoing services.

4 Women's centers will provide information, guidance, and referrals and will often accompany the victims to the appropriate agencies.

5 Family counseling agencies will provide someone to talk things over with, as well as information, referrals, counseling, and discussion groups. Here too, they will often provide someone to accompany the victim to the appropriate agencies.

Part 2

Safety on the job

Preventing accidents and crime on the job is slightly different from preventing them at home. To a large extent, the responsibility for security and occupational health rests with the employer. However, it is the employee's responsibility to cooperate with safety and accident-reducing precautions and to report safety hazards when they appear. Accidents can and do happen in the best of industrial plants and even in the most well-run offices. Everyone in the workplace can and should take as many precautions as possible to avoid them. An employer should be especially aware of all his or her responsibilities to employees and of the steps that can be taken to minimize the risk of accidents.

Self-assessment

IF YOU WORK IN AN OFFICE, DO YOU:

	YES	NO
■ Keep debris off the floor in your office or work area?	_____	_____
■ Store scissors with points down in an easily accessible place (not in a drawer) to avoid accidental cuts or punctures?	_____	_____
■ Keep cords for typewriters, lamps, pencil sharpeners flush with the wall to avoid falling or tripping over them?	_____	_____
■ In general, keep your work area neat and clean?	_____	_____
■ Know where the fire extinguishers are located and how to use them properly?	_____	_____
■ Know where and how to turn in a fire alarm?	_____	_____
■ Know where the emergency exits are located?	_____	_____
■ Know proper emergency procedure in case of elevator failure?	_____	_____
■ Know the proper way to dispose of flammable waste?	_____	_____
■ Know the proper use of machinery, such as copying machines, shredders, or lithograph equipment, in your office?	_____	_____
■ Know the regulations governing smoking in your office?	_____	_____
■ Know the current fire-emergency plan in your office?	_____	_____
■ When using a file cabinet, open one drawer at a time to avoid tipping the entire cabinet?	_____	_____
■ Make sure that books or heavy objects stored on shelves are securely placed?	_____	_____
■ Avoid smoking in areas where there are many papers, such as in a record room?	_____	_____
■ Use large ashtrays for cigarettes, pipes, and cigars?	_____	_____

	YES	NO
■ Never drop ashes into a wastebasket?	____	____
■ Avoid leaving the coffeepot plugged in overnight?	____	____
■ Avoid overloading electrical outlets?	____	____
■ Pull on the plug to disconnect a wire instead of yanking the cord?	____	____

IF YOU WORK IN AN INDUSTRIAL PLANT, DO YOU:

- ■ Keep aisles free of materials that can interfere with the movement of power trucks or fire equipment?
- ■ Store tools properly and put them back when you have finished working with them?
- ■ Check that power tools are double-insulated or grounded before using them?
- ■ Avoid overloading a hand truck and check that a load is stable before moving the truck?
- ■ When using a hand truck, avoid piling a load so high that it blocks your view?
- ■ Stand clear of cranes, suspended loads, or overhead work?
- ■ Stand clear when you hear warning bells or horns from power trucks or overhead equipment?
- ■ Keep away from barricaded areas?
- ■ Wear required protective equipment and clothing, such as safety glasses, hard hat, safety shoes, and earplugs?
- ■ Make sure that tools or materials are securely stored?
- ■ Operate machinery only when all safeguards are in place?
- ■ Keep clear of moving parts on machinery?

Self-assessment
(continued)

INDUSTRIAL PLANT (continued)

	YES	NO
■ Turn off machines when you clean them or fix them?	_____	_____
■ Avoid leaving a running machine unattended?	_____	_____
■ Use a machine only the way it is designed to be used and only when you are sure you know how?	_____	_____
■ Obey all safety rules and signs at all times?	_____	_____
■ Follow instructions, or if you are not sure of the safe procedure, ask your supervisor?	_____	_____
■ Correct unsafe conditions or report them to a supervisor immediately?	_____	_____
■ Know how to get first aid for yourself or a fellow worker?	_____	_____
■ Adjust or repair equipment only if you are qualified or authorized to do so?	_____	_____
■ Use the right tool for each job and use it correctly and safely?	_____	_____
■ Avoid carrying sharp or pointed tools, such as screwdrivers, in your pocket?	_____	_____
■ Get help to lift heavy loads?	_____	_____
■ Avoid horseplay on the job?	_____	_____
■ Obey the smoking regulations within your work space?	_____	_____
■ Keep your cigarettes and food away from the work area, especially if you work with chemicals?	_____	_____

FOR THE EMPLOYER, DO YOU:

■ Provide a workplace free of hazards?	_____	_____
■ Familiarize yourself with mandatory safety standards pertaining to your business or industry?	_____	_____

	YES	NO
■ Make sure your employees are aware of all safety standards?	___	___
■ Inform your employees about the Occupational Safety and Health Administration (OSHA)?	___	___
■ Examine conditions in your workplace to make sure they conform with safety standards?	___	___
■ Remove or guard hazardous areas?	___	___
■ Make sure employees use safe tools, safe equipment, and any required protective clothing?	___	___
■ Use color codes, signs, or posters to warn employees of hazards?	___	___
■ Establish and periodically update specific and clear operating procedures for all equipment?	___	___
■ Provide medical exams for employees?	___	___
■ Retain records of all work-related injuries and illnesses?	___	___
■ Post signs in the workplace informing employees of their rights and responsibilities?	___	___
■ Post violations of safety standards at the work site?	___	___
■ Keep hallway bathrooms locked?	___	___
■ Equip hallway doors with peepholes?	___	___
■ Keep utility closets locked?	___	___
■ Install closed-circuit televison monitors in hallways or other areas that require tight security?	___	___
■ Make sure all entrance and exit areas are well lighted?	___	___
■ Equip each elevator with a bypass switch that will prevent it from stopping on floors where offices are closed?	___	___

Self-assessment
(continued)

EMPLOYER (continued)

	YES	NO
■ Equip each elevator with a mirror so that a person can observe the inside before entering?	_____	_____
■ Bolt machines such as typewriters to their desks or tables?	_____	_____
■ Have identification numbers etched onto all pieces of office machinery?	_____	_____
■ Keep valuable files and portfolios in locked, fireproof metal cabinets?	_____	_____
■ Log and mark "for deposit in account of ——" on all checks as soon as they are received?	_____	_____
■ Run security checks each night to make sure no one is hiding in the building?	_____	_____
■ Store all blank checks in a safe?	_____	_____
■ Lock up postage meters and check-writing equipment when the office is closed?	_____	_____
■ Know what to do if your office is burglarized?	_____	_____
■ Know what to do if you are the victim of a holdup?	_____	_____

FOR THE EMPLOYEE, DO YOU:

■ Follow all your employer's safety and health standards and rules?	_____	_____
■ Wear and use all prescribed protective equipment and clothing?	_____	_____
■ Report hazardous conditions to your supervisor?	_____	_____
■ Report any job-related injuries or illnesses to your employer and seek treatment promptly?	_____	_____
■ Know your rights as an employee?	_____	_____
■ Know about OSHA and what it requires of employers?	_____	_____

	YES	NO
■ Know where you can get information about OSHA?	____	____
■ Use the buddy system when traveling through lonely areas of the building or after working hours?	____	____
■ Keep the doors locked if you are working in an office alone?	____	____
■ Refuse to give the addresses or telephone numbers of other employees to strangers?	____	____
■ Stand near the control panel when riding in an elevator?	____	____
■ Inform the security guard or police if you notice a suspicious-looking person on the premises?	____	____
■ Always wear your employee-identification card if it is required?	____	____
■ Avoid leaving valuables in an unlocked desk or locker?	____	____
■ Habitually safeguard your pocketbook or wallet?	____	____
■ Safeguard your credit cards and report their loss immediately?	____	____
■ Keep a current list of all credit cards and numbers in a secure location at home?	____	____
■ Avoid carrying excessive cash while at work?	____	____
■ Take special precautions to protect your paycheck?	____	____
■ Refuse to let anyone remove machinery from your office unless he gives proper identification?	____	____
■ Safeguard your luggage if you are leaving on a trip directly from work?	____	____
■ Insist that some type of silent robbery-alarm system be installed if your job requires that you handle cash?	____	____

□ Safety in the office

The office is a place not often associated with danger. However, accidents can occur: electric shock from defective office machinery, falls and scrapes from carelessly opened drawers, fire from a thoughtlessly discarded cigarette.

Most minor accidents in the office result from untidiness. The office should be kept as neat as possible. In general, books should be stored on shelves; pencils, scissors, letter openers, and other sharp objects should be kept in holders made for them; and furniture should be kept in its place. Don't leave chairs pulled out or drawers gaping.

Falls, resulting in scrapes, sprains, and fractures, are the most common office accidents. Often they are caused by this very kind of untidiness: scrambled cords, boxes in the hall, and slippery floors. Keep your office and halls, entryways, and lobbies as neat as possible to avoid accidents.

Back injury is another common office injury. When lifting boxes or parcels, size up the load realistically. Do not lift more than you can handle comfortably. Place yourself directly in front of the object, with your feet evenly spaced apart. Bend your knees so that most of the lifting force comes from your legs, not your back. If an object looks too heavy, get help. Don't try to lift and carry it yourself.

In general, exercise caution throughout the office. Walk, don't run, in hallways, down stairs, through doorways, and around corners. Be tidy: pick up pencils, close drawers, wipe up spills. Don't climb on office furniture. Keep a small footstool handy for reaching high places. Finally, don't adopt that classic office posture: leaning back in the chair with your feet on the desk. It may be comfortable; it may even make you feel powerful; but it is dangerous.

ELECTRIC SHOCK

In these days of electric typewriters, pencil sharpeners, copy machines, Telexes, and shredders, the chances of injury from electric shock are great. Watch for frayed wires, broken equipment, and water on the floor. These can all cause shock—and, particularly with more powerful machinery, severe injury.

Overloaded circuits are another problem. Not only can overtaxed circuits result in electric shock, but they can cause fires.

OFFICE FIRES

Carelessly discarded or overlooked cigarettes are probably the major cause of office fires. Use a large ashtray when working at a desk and never smoke in file rooms or other areas where highly combustible papers are stored.

Know the fire-drill rules of your office. Be sure evacuation procedures are clear in your mind; most particularly, be sure you know where the fire exits are located. Make it a point to know how to turn in an alarm. When reporting a fire, be clear in your directions.

Read carefully the labels on the fire extinguishers in your office. Know where all extinguishers are located in your office and learn how to use them.

FIRST AID IN THE OFFICE

Most large offices have medical areas with staff doctors and nurses; however, if you work in a small office that does not have such a service, make sure a complete first-aid kit is located in a central place. If no doctor or nurse is on staff, check that an employee trained in first aid is at hand. If you realize that first-aid measures in your office are inadequate, speak to the personnel officer about setting up such a service.

☐ Safety in the industrial plant

Specific safety rules will vary according to the type of industrial plant you work in. For example, the safeguards surrounding a chemical plant will be quite different from those surrounding an auto-repair shop. Learn about the *specific* safety rules that apply to your industry and your particular plant. Signs, rule books, and guidance from personnel officers are usually provided; if they are not, do something about the lack. Make sure you are aware of all safety measures and speak to a supervisor about informing other employees. The final responsibility for safety rests with *you*. No matter how many rules and requirements exist, they will not be effective unless you follow them.

The careless use of machinery is the primary cause of accidents in industrial plants. Forklift trucks, for example, are frequently involved. Often they are loaded improperly (either without attention to balance or with loads that are too large) or driven carelessly (either too fast or with too many stops and turns). If you must operate any motor vehicle in your plant, learn not only the correct way to operate it, but also the special safety conditions for its use.

Many other types of heavy machinery cause safety problems. Large overhead machines can be a major source of danger. Never work underneath one; if you work at one, take care that tools or other work materials do not fall.

Know the machine you operate and use it carefully. Keep guards or protective devices in place. Never walk away leaving a machine running. Keep fingers, loose clothing, and jewelry out of and away from moving parts. Wear comfortable, well-fitting clothes when you're working; and more important, wear any required safety equipment, such as hard hat, goggles, earplugs, or mask.

With small hand tools such as screwdrivers, take equal care. Use only the precise tool for the precise job. Check all tools before using them and repair damaged ones. Never carry small tools in a pocket; if you slip and fall you could be stabbed or cut. Instead, use a tool kit or belt.

INDUSTRIAL FIRES

Fires are frequently a problem in industrial workplaces, particularly in chemical plants. Learn all rules in your plant with regard to fire prevention. Know how to report a fire quickly and efficiently. Learn where extinguishers are located so that you can effectively douse a small fire in your area.

THE OCCUPATIONAL SAFETY AND HEALTH ACT

The Occupational Safety and Health Act of 1970 is the federal law that affects your safety and the safety and health conditions in your workplace. Administered by the Occupational Safety and Health Administration (OSHA) of the U.S. Department of Labor, this act is designed to encourage employers to reduce hazards in the workplace and to improve existing safety and health programs. The act requires each employer to comply with federal occupational safety and health standards. In addition, OSHA conducts inspections of offices and plants to determine that standards are being met.

The act also provides employees with certain rights. For example, as an employee, you have the right to obtain information from your employer on safety and health hazards. In addition, if you believe hazardous conditions exist, you can request the OSHA area director to conduct an inspection.

For further information, get in touch with your regional OSHA office. Personnel in that office will clarify your rights and responsibilities under the law and are prepared to help with occupational health problems. (See the list of regional OSHA offices on pages 101–04.)

☐ Special tips for the employer

As an employer, you are responsible for providing the safest and healthiest working environment you can for your employees. Responsibilities will vary according to the kind of office or plant you supervise, but, in general, a number of standards remain constant for an accident-free, crime-free place of employment.

- Make sure entrances to the building are well lighted, including alleys surrounding the building and the rear of the building.

- Make sure night lights are left on inside the building.

- Install dead-bolt locks and sturdy doors to the outside entryways and to doorways to common halls.

- Make sure windows are protected with locking devices and security bars, if necessary.

- Install a burglar-alarm system or employ a guard service.

- Equip each elevator with a bypass switch to ensure that the elevator will not stop at unoccupied floors.

- Equip each elevator with a mirror so that employees can see the inside before entering.

- Make sure that sufficient fire extinguishers are provided and that a fire-escape system has been devised and publicized.

- Provide a first-aid center of some kind. In a small office, make sure that a complete first-aid kit is on the premises and that at least one supervising person knows first-aid techniques.

- Devise a training plan to teach employees about the safety rules of your office or plant. Provide refresher courses at least once a year.

□ Crime on the job

To prevent burglary or mugging in an office or plant, follow many of the same rules you use for protecting your house. Read over Chapters 6 and 7, "Crime Prevention Around the House" and "Crime Prevention for Yourself," and apply them to your working environment and your working life.

IN CASE OF A HOLDUP

Despite responsible efforts at crime prevention, burglaries, muggings, and holdups can occur. If you are held up, try to remain calm. Criminals may be easily provoked or may be under the influence of drugs. Remain defensive; do not try to attack a burglar. Take a good look at the holdup person: note weight, height, and any peculiarities such as tattoos, scars, or moles. In addition, take note of the weapon so you can describe it later to police. Watch for your attacker to touch something, and then pre-serve the object (a telephone receiver, a pencil) for fingerprints. Get a description of any vehicle the holdup person uses to escape and write down the license number.

Notify the police as soon as you can. Give the precise location, including the room number, if necessary. Remember, do not try to fight off the intruder. It is safer to allow your money and valuables to be taken. They're almost always replaceable.

IN CASE OF BURGLARY

If you find that your office or plant has been burglarized, telephone the police immediately. Instruct all co-workers to leave the scene and keep it undisturbed. Fingerprints and other revealing evidence can be found only if the room or office is exactly as the burglar left it. Assist the police in tracking down all missing items.

Part 3

Safety on the road

Automobile accidents take more lives each year than any other kind of accident. As we have observed regarding accidents in other areas of our lives, accidents on the road can be prevented. In general, road accidents occur for one of three reasons: the driver's insufficient knowledge of the vehicle itself; the driver's lack of respect for the conditions of the road; and the driver's carelessness with regard to driving when he is physically unfit to do so—because of physical illness, the side effects of medication, or the overuse of alcohol or other drugs.

Self-assessment

AS A DRIVER, DO YOU:

	YES	NO
■ Keep the rear window ledge clear of clothing, books, or other obstructions?	_____	_____
■ Avoid overloading the car?	_____	_____
■ Keep a window partly open when driving with the heater on?	_____	_____
■ Keep objects off the dashboard and away from the rear-view mirror?	_____	_____
■ Keep brakes, windshield wipers, steering, and other equipment in good repair?	_____	_____
■ Have the oil, water, and tires (including the spare) checked before going on a trip?	_____	_____
■ Check that all signals (including brake lights) are in proper working condition at all times?	_____	_____
■ Make sure your windshield wipers are in good working order?	_____	_____
■ Check side and rear-view mirrors each time you use the car?	_____	_____
■ Have your heater and air conditioner checked so that they are in proper working order?	_____	_____
■ Know what it means when your brakes develop a screeching sound?	_____	_____
■ Have brake linings and wheel balance checked regularly?	_____	_____
■ Check that tires are inflated to proper pressure?	_____	_____
■ Have flares in your car to use in an emergency?	_____	_____
■ Keep jumper cables in your car in case the battery dies?	_____	_____
■ Have electrical tape to repair leaky engine hoses in your car?	_____	_____
■ Feel physically well, mentally alert, and calm before driving?	_____	_____

	YES	NO
■ Know and observe the rules of the road? Know specifically the driving laws of the areas you may be traveling in?	_____	_____
■ Remain calm in heavy traffic?	_____	_____
■ Know what to do in case your car breaks down?	_____	_____
■ Know how to handle a skid?	_____	_____
■ Pull off the road when changing a tire?	_____	_____
■ Refrain from picking up hitchhikers?	_____	_____
■ Avoid sudden stops?	_____	_____
■ Drive within the speed limit?	_____	_____
■ Watch for pedestrians (especially children) darting into the road from between parked cars?	_____	_____
■ Watch out for children on bicycles, sleds, scooters, roller skates, or other fast toys?	_____	_____
■ Merge smoothly with the traffic stream and avoid coming to a stop when entering an expressway or making another merger?	_____	_____
■ Move to the left at such points as entrances, exits, and service areas?	_____	_____
■ Signal every time you wish to pass or change lanes?	_____	_____
■ Plan your exit from an expressway well in advance and slow down on the exit ramp?	_____	_____
■ Pull off the road to read a road map?	_____	_____
■ Avoid driving with an unrestrained dog or cat in the car?	_____	_____
■ Use safety restraining devices, such as car seats and harnesses, for younger children?	_____	_____
■ Use seat belts at all times and insist that your passengers do too?	_____	_____

Self-assessment
(continued)

DRIVER (continued)

	YES	NO
■ Avoid driving after taking medication that might affect your alertness or sight?	____	____
■ Avoid driving if you have been drinking?	____	____
■ Avoid driving if you are tired?	____	____
■ Insist that children ride in the back seat of the car?	____	____
■ Know your destination and the precise route before you start a trip?	____	____
■ Keep a first-aid kit in the glove compartment?	____	____
■ Keep a blanket in the trunk?	____	____
■ Carry a flashlight in the glove compartment?	____	____
■ Use proper signals when turning, changing lanes, or stopping?	____	____
■ Turn on low-beam lights when driving in fog or snow?	____	____
■ Turn down your brights when approaching another car?	____	____
■ Check carefully behind the car for objects or people (especially children) before backing out of a driveway?	____	____
■ Before entering your car, check the back seat for an intruder?	____	____
■ Whenever possible, travel on well-lighted and well-populated streets?	____	____
■ Close car windows and lock doors whenever you park your car?	____	____
■ Always lock car doors when you are riding in the car?	____	____
■ Keep your car in gear while stopped at a traffic light or stop sign?	____	____
■ Check your rear-view mirror frequently to make sure another car is not following you?	____	____

	YES	NO
■ Sound the horn to get the attention of neighbors if you are approached by a suspicious-looking person?	___	___
■ When parking your car at night, select a well-lighted place?	___	___
■ Check for loiterers before leaving your car?	___	___
■ Make sure never to leave car keys in the ignition, even if you are parked for only a short time?	___	___

AS A PEDESTRIAN, DO YOU:

	YES	NO
■ When walking home at night, check to be sure you are not being followed?	___	___
■ Walk near the curb and avoid passing close to shrubbery, dark doorways, and alleys—especially at night?	___	___
■ When returning home by taxi, ask the driver to wait until you are safely inside?	___	___
■ Cross the street at the corner rather than at midblock?	___	___
■ Start crossing at the beginning of the green light for maximum crossing time?	___	___
■ Keep going if the signal "don't walk" starts to flash after you have started to cross the street?	___	___
■ Look both ways before crossing a street?	___	___
■ Avoid crossing between parked cars?	___	___
■ Watch for turning vehicles and for unexpected moves by drivers?	___	___
■ Wear something light in color or carry a flashlight or reflector when walking at night so that drivers can see you?	___	___

☐ Safe driving and the condition of your car

Perhaps the most basic rule for safe driving is to keep your car in good running condition at all times and respect its mechanical power and limitations. Mechanical problems such as defects in brakes and wheel balance can result in a dangerous skid; incorrect pressure in your tires can cause a blowout. Have your car checked at regular intervals—every three months is best—to make sure it works perfectly.

Be sure you use all safety devices provided in your car. It is the law for all automobiles in the United States to be manufactured with safety belts. Get into the habit of putting on your seat belt whenever you drive or ride in your car, and make sure passengers buckle up too. Three out of four fatal accidents happen within 25 miles of home; yet short trips around town are precisely the ones during which drivers neglect to use safety belts. For infants and young children, be sure to use approved car seats and harnesses. Insist that lively children ride in the back seat of the car at all times.

Other safety devices such as emergency brakes and blinker lights should be in good working condition. When having your car checked, make sure the mechanic pays special attention to these important safety measures. Disc brakes have a screech alarm that sounds when the brake lining has to be replaced. When you apply pressure to the brake pedal, the sound goes off. Do not ignore this important warning.

Make sure you and members of your family are expert drivers before taking a car out on the road. Many high schools and adult-education centers offer driver-training courses, and new drivers should take the courses. (In some states, insurance rates are lower if a driver is a graduate of such a course.) Know the driving laws of your state and abide by them.

When traveling on a superhighway, be aware of basic highway snares and know how to avoid them. Learn to merge quickly. Move left at decision points, such as entrances, exits, service areas, and turns. Signal all passes and lane changes. Know what to do if your car stalls in traffic. And, of course, observe all speed limits.

If your car stalls or breaks down, get off the highway onto the shoulder of the road. If you cannot repair the defect, raise the car's hood and trunk and tie a handkerchief to the antenna or door handle. Switch on the four-way flasher. If the car breaks down at night, turn on the low beams and the interior lights. Avoid using turn signals when the car is stopped; they can be confusing to other drivers. Carry flares and use them in such an emergency. Stay near your car and wait for help.

If your car goes into a skid, don't slam on the brakes. Slowly take your foot off the gas and turn the wheel *into* the skid to straighten out the car and help retain traction. If the car snaps back too fast, whip the steering wheel back in the opposite direction.

☐ Safe driving and the condition of the road

When weather or road conditions are dangerous, avoid driving if possible. If you must drive, know how to handle hazards caused by rain, fog, ice, and snow.

In rain, reduce speed, turn on headlights to low beam, and allow extra car lengths for stopping. Watch for pedestrians; in rain, people often walk with their heads down, their vision is obstructed by umbrellas, and their hearing is impaired by wind and rain. When driving through deep water, slow down and shift to a lower gear to prevent stalling. Lightly ride your brakes to keep them dried out.

In fog, the first rule is to slow down. Keep headlights on low beam to avoid blinding oncoming drivers and watch the side of the road to make sure you are in the correct lane. Be extra careful when entering a patch of fog; an accident may have occurred just ahead.

In snow and ice, always use snow tires, studded tires, or reinforced chains. Slow down and take measures to keep your windshield and windows clear. Slippery surfaces require longer stopping distances. Test your brakes frequently to get a feel for the road.

☐ Safe driving and your health

Your health and state of mind directly affect your driving skills. You should be physically well and mentally alert—always—when driving. If you are feeling sleepy, get off the road, lock your car, and take a nap. Many highways have rest areas; don't hesitate to use them.

When planning a long trip, know how to avoid drowsiness. Begin your trip when you are well rested—not after a day's work. Stop every two or three hours to stretch your muscles and have coffee or a light snack. Stop driving the moment you feel drowsy. Keep the car well ventilated and do not use drugs that profess to keep you awake.

Certain medications, such as cold remedies and many prescription drugs, can cause drowsiness, blurred vision, or other hazards to driving. If you have taken medication that interferes with your driving ability, do not drive under any circumstances. If you have taken medication you have not used before, wait until you know how it will affect you before trying to drive.

Driving after drinking is the major cause of death on the road. Statistics show that approximately 50,000 people are killed each year in traffic accidents, and drinking is a factor in at least half these cases. Alcohol impairs judgment and coordination and thus causes driving performance to deteriorate.

The concentration of alcohol depends on the number and strength of the drinks you've had, the time elapsed since drinking, your body weight, and the quantity and kind of food in your stomach. If you have had more than three drinks (and in many cases less), no amount of black coffee, cold showers, fresh air, or exercise will affect the intoxication. You must wait until the alcohol wears off. And only then should you drive.

☐ Preventing crime on the road

When driving in a dangerous neighborhood or at night, make certain your car doors are locked and the windows are rolled up to where a mugger cannot insert his arm. If you are assaulted in your car, hold down your horn and drive away quickly.

If you believe you are being followed by another car, do not drive into your driveway or park in a deserted area. Pull over to the curb in a spot where people are circulating. Let the suspicious-looking car pass by. If the stranger persists in following you, drive to a gas station, police station, or other place where you can get help.

If you are followed into your driveway at night, stay in your car with doors locked until you can identify the occupants of the strange car or can determine their intent. Sound the horn to get the attention of neighbors or to scare off the intruders.

Muggers often wait in parked cars. Always lock your car when you leave it parked and check the back seat before getting in. At night, always park in a lighted area.

☐ Safety tips for the pedestrian

Contrary to popular belief, pedestrians do not always have the legal right-of-way in traffic. The laws are clear: pedestrians have the right-of-way at a crosswalk with no traffic light; pedestrians have the right-of-way at a crosswalk *with* a traffic light, so long as the light is green, *not* red. In any case, never rely totally on a traffic light. Walk defensively; watch for careless drivers.

Do not jaywalk. Jaywalking means crossing a street at any point except a corner, crossing against a light, or veering off a direct course in a heedless way. In many cities, jaywalking is a traffic violation. It is also dangerous.

SPECIAL TIPS FOR WOMEN PEDESTRIANS

Women are often targets for crime on the streets. Muggings, purse snatchings, and rape are dangers to be guarded against with utmost care.

If you suspect someone is following you, cross the street. If he persists, prepare to scream or run—or both. Try to make your way to a residence or a shop; if necessary, flag down a passing car. Make it a habit to carry an aerosol noisemaking device for protection. If you are threatened by a driver, scream and run in the direction opposite from the way the car is headed. This way, the driver will have to turn around to pursue you. Always walk near the curb. Avoid shortcuts through backyards, alleyways, or dark streets. (See also Chapter 7, "Crime Prevention for Yourself.")

Part **4**

Safety at play

Despite what we would like to think, when we are at play the opportunity for accidents often goes *up* rather than down. We are relaxed, getting away from it all, at ease. Our defenses are down, and as a result, we often become careless. Every sport or form of recreation has its hazards. Golfers, joggers, tennis players, and bird watchers must all take certain precautions to prevent injury or accident. It is important to know the safety rules of whatever game or recreational activity you are involved in. Beware, be careful, and play safely.

Certain sports are particularly dangerous and have a high incidence of injury. It is those that we will look at here.

Self-assessment

WHEN CAMPING AND HIKING, DO YOU:

	YES	NO
▪ Tell someone who is not going on the hike where you are headed and when you expect to return?	___	___
▪ Allow sufficient time to reach your campsite before dark?	___	___
▪ Make sure you extinguish cigarettes and matches completely before discarding them?	___	___
▪ Plan your travel route carefully to avoid getting lost in the woods?	___	___
▪ Take along proper clothing and equipment, including a compass, a transistor radio, and sturdy boots?	___	___
▪ Keep alert for loose rocks, ledges, and other natural hazards?	___	___
▪ Keep careful track of time and weather?	___	___
▪ Know how to start a fire and keep it going safely?	___	___
▪ Make sure you extinguish fires completely before breaking camp?	___	___
▪ Avoid overtaxing yourself physically while hiking?	___	___
▪ Know what to do if you get lost?	___	___
▪ Know that exposure to rain, snow, heat, or cold is more dangerous than hunger or thirst?	___	___
▪ Know what to do in case of injury?	___	___
▪ Know where to look for water?	___	___
▪ Know the universal call for help?	___	___

WHEN HUNTING, DO YOU:

▪ Handle every gun as if it were loaded and never point it at anything unless you intend to shoot?	___	___
▪ Make sure your gun is unloaded when it is not in use?	___	___

	YES	NO

- Carry your gun with the muzzle pointed up? _____ _____
- Leave the safety catch of your gun *on* until just before shooting? _____ _____
- Slip shells out, break the action, or hand your gun to a companion while you climb a fence or jump a ditch? _____ _____
- Stay abreast of your companions? _____ _____
- Make sure the gun barrel is not plugged with dirt or snow? _____ _____
- Check that you have the correct ammunition? _____ _____
- See your quarry plainly before firing? _____ _____
- Obey all game laws? _____ _____
- Know the best color to wear for hunting? _____ _____
- Know how to avoid being accidentally shot? _____ _____

WHEN BOATING, DO YOU:

- Avoid overloading your boat? _____ _____
- Check the weather-bureau forecast before taking your boat onto open water? _____ _____
- Equip your boat with at least the following safety items:

  Proper lights? _____ _____

  Lifesaving gear? _____ _____

  An anchor? _____ _____

  Oars? _____ _____

  A boat hook? _____ _____

  Extra line? _____ _____

  A fire extinguisher? _____ _____

  A tool kit? _____ _____

  A first-aid kit? _____ _____

Self-assessment
(continued)

BOATING (continued)

	YES	NO
■ Know water-traffic rules before taking out a boat?	———	———
■ Know what to do if your boat is swamped or overturns?	———	———
■ Know how to handle a boat expertly before taking it out alone?	———	———
■ Never permit children to take a boat out alone unless they are expert seamen?	———	———

WHEN SWIMMING, DO YOU:

■ Avoid swimming right after eating?	———	———
■ Avoid swimming alone?	———	———
■ Swim only in areas guarded by experienced lifeguards?	———	———
■ Never let children swim without adult supervision?	———	———
■ Practice your lifesaving skills once a year?	———	———
■ Make sure you are a good swimmer before heading into deep or difficult water?	———	———
■ Know that white water is particularly dangerous for swimming?	———	———
■ Keep aware of undertows, fast currents, and whirlpools when swimming in natural water?	———	———
■ Keep aware of the presence of dangerous marine life, especially when swimming in unfamiliar water?	———	———

IF YOU HAVE A POOL, DO YOU:

■ Avoid swimming in the area directly under the diving board?	———	———
■ Take precautions against falls on slippery walkways, decks, diving boards, or ladders?	———	———

	YES	NO

- Look out for shallow water and avoid jumping or diving into it? _____ _____

- Watch out for protruding water pipes, ladders, or other sharp objects that may cause injury? _____ _____

- Watch out for wiring that might cause shock if touched with wet hands? _____ _____

- Make sure the pool area is adequately protected against easy access by unsupervised children? _____ _____

WHEN BICYCLING, DO YOU:

- Obey all traffic regulations, signs, signals, and markings? _____ _____

- Avoid congested streets and use bicycle lanes or paths where possible? _____ _____

- Keep right and ride *with* traffic, not against it? _____ _____

- Keep as close to the curb as possible and ride in single file? _____ _____

- Watch for opening doors on parked cars and for cars pulling into traffic? _____ _____

- Use hand signals? _____ _____

- Leave plenty of room for other vehicles to pass? _____ _____

- Ride your bike defensively? _____ _____

- Watch for cars making right turns? (Drivers may not see you.) _____ _____

- Exercise extreme care at intersections, especially when making a left turn? _____ _____

- Avoid stopping short? _____ _____

Self-assessment
(continued)

BICYCLING (continued)

	YES	NO
■ Apply equal pressure on hand brakes so that both wheels will brake evenly?	____	____
■ Protect your bike by locking it whenever you leave it unattended?	____	____
■ When you are coasting on a bike with foot brakes, put the pedals in a level position for a quick stop when coming to an intersection?	____	____
■ Watch out for pedestrians?	____	____
■ Install reflectors and lights for riding your bike at night?	____	____
■ Inspect the following parts on your bicycle regularly:	____	____
Brakes?	____	____
Pedals?	____	____
Lights?	____	____
Reflectors?	____	____
Shifting mechanisms?	____	____
Horn or other warning devices?	____	____
Tires and spokes?	____	____
Saddle?	____	____
Handlebars?	____	____
All nuts and bolts?	____	____
■ Avoid the common road hazards, such as sewer grates, potholes, loose sand or gravel, and man-hole covers?	____	____
■ Know how to select a bicycle of the correct size, weight, and mechanical complexity for yourself or your child?	____	____

WHEN SKIING, DO YOU:

	YES	NO
■ Secure professional ski instruction, especially if you are a beginner?	_____	_____
■ Avoid skiing on runs that are beyond your ability?	_____	_____
■ When entering a trail or slope from a side or intersecting trail, check for approaching skiers?	_____	_____
■ When standing, check for approaching skiers before resuming your run?	_____	_____
■ When walking or climbing in a ski area, keep to the side of the trail or slope?	_____	_____
■ Keep off closed trails?	_____	_____
■ Avoid stopping where you may obstruct the loading or unloading of a lift?	_____	_____
■ Avoid stopping where you cannot be seen from above?	_____	_____
■ Make sure you are in topnotch physical condition before attempting strenuous skiing?	_____	_____
■ Have your ski equipment checked regularly by a professional for proper fit and maintenance?	_____	_____
■ Wear proper clothing to protect you against the elements?	_____	_____
■ Wear safety straps to prevent your skis from running away if you fall?	_____	_____
■ Avoid wearing loose clothing, such as a long scarf, which can become entangled in a lift, tow rope, or ski poles?	_____	_____
■ Ski only with boots that fit perfectly?	_____	_____
■ Have only the best bindings and know how to check that they are in perfect working order?	_____	_____
■ Know how to maintain your ski equipment?	_____	_____

Self-assessment
(continued)

WHEN SLEDDING AND TOBOGGANING, DO YOU:

	YES	NO
■ Avoid pushing, shoving, or other horseplay while using a sled, toboggan, or snow disk?	_____	_____
■ Hold tie ropes on top of the vehicle to prevent ropes from slipping underneath the sled and causing an abrupt stop?	_____	_____
■ Avoid sliding through traffic intersections or across streets?	_____	_____
■ Check sled for easy steering?	_____	_____
■ Move off a busy slope quickly when you reach the bottom to avoid being struck by those following you?	_____	_____
■ Choose a sled with a protective guard or bumper to prevent cuts and other injuries in a collision?	_____	_____
■ Avoid equipment with sharp, jagged edges?	_____	_____
■ Check the slope for poor conditions, such as bare spots, ruts, rocks, tree stumps, before riding down it?	_____	_____
■ Know how to stop the vehicle or get off safely in an emergency?	_____	_____
■ Know how to keep a sled or toboggan in good repair?	_____	_____

WHEN SNOWMOBILING, DO YOU:

	YES	NO
■ Use normal driving sense: avoid tailgating, signal your direction to other drivers, and control speed according to conditions?	_____	_____
■ Know how to operate and drive a snowmobile with confidence before taking it out?	_____	_____

	YES	NO

- Use extra caution when driving a snowmobile at night? _____ _____

- Avoid snowmobiling on unfamiliar terrain? _____ _____

- Refrain from jumping or doing other stunts with your snowmobile? _____ _____

- Use the buddy system when snowmobiling so that if an accident occurs your companion can seek help? _____ _____

- Watch the path ahead to avoid obstacles such as rocks, trees, fences, and ditches? _____ _____

- Avoid snowmobiling in bad weather? _____ _____

- Know and follow traffic laws and regulations for snowmobiles in your area? _____ _____

WHEN ICE SKATING, DO YOU:

- Avoid skating alone? _____ _____

- Avoid skating on an unfamiliar pond? _____ _____

- Avoid skating at night unless the rink or pond is adequately lighted? _____ _____

- Stop skating before you become overly fatigued and careless? _____ _____

- Skate only on a surface that is free of snow or rubble? _____ _____

- Skate only when the ice is thick enough? _____ _____

- Wear skates that fit properly and are sharp? _____ _____

- Cover blades with safety guards when not in use, particularly when you are carrying your skates? _____ _____

□ Camping and hiking

The first tip for danger-free camping and hiking is to start out on an excursion *prepared.* Be sure to take proper clothing, particularly proper hiking shoes or boots. Take clothing suitable to the weather and be ready for a sudden storm, heat wave, or chill. Carry all essential equipment, including matches, in waterproof containers. If you are camping, know the correct and safest type of cooking equipment and shelter gear, but take precautions against overloading your pack. Always carry a map, compass, and knife. It's also a good idea to carry a whistle. Before heading off on your trip, be sure someone at home knows approximately where you will be and when you plan to return.

If you get lost, remain calm. Decide (based on weather, time of day, and general knowledge of the terrain) whether you should stay put or push on. If you stay where you are, make a shelter. Build a signal fire to attract the attention of forest rangers. If you proceed, leave a marker of some kind, such as a pile of stones, to guide the rescue team. Go slowly and carefully. Try to find a high point with a good view. Plan your route carefully.

Know the *universal call for help:* three signals in rapid succession repeated at regular intervals. These can be three shots, three flashes of light, three blasts of a whistle, or three puffs of smoke. Help will come.

If you are a novice hiker or camper, take along a guide or an experienced person on the first few outings you make. You'll learn proper outdoor methods and you'll be in far less danger.

□ Hunting

Hunting is a very sophisticated sport, and it can be a deadly one. Because the shotgun requires the utmost care in use, know precisely what you are doing before you begin a hunting trip. If you are a novice, hunt with an expert.

A number of rules should be followed with regard to using a shotgun: never keep a loaded or uncased gun in your car; never prop a loaded gun against another object, such as a car or a tree stump; never wander in front of or behind fellow hunters—stay with them and make noise when you are under cover; never shoot randomly at movement or sound; never shoot at game over the rise of a hill. At home, store your shotgun in a locked case or cabinet (see "Firearms," page 20).

Hunters often camp out. Be sure you are as expert a camper as you are a hunter. A hunter is as likely to be injured resting after the hunting day as he is while actually practicing his sport.

☐ Boating

Operating a boat, be it canoe, motorboat, Sunfish, day sailor, or any of innumerable larger craft, is as serious—and dangerous—as operating an automobile. No one should operate a boat who is not totally knowledgeable about the particular type he is operating. The person in charge of a sophisticated boat, such as a large sailboat or motorcraft, should be a graduate of an accredited training course. Children should be accompanied by an adult whenever they take out a boat, no matter how small the craft.

In addition to knowing the boat, it is imperative to know the rules of boating. Especially at the height of the summer season, traffic on the water can be thick and dangerous. Anyone who does not know water-safety rules is a menace not only to himself but to other boaters.

In general, know the load capacity of your boat, and never overload it. Make sure the weight of passengers and supplies is balanced, particularly in a sailboat.

Know your cruise plan before you begin a trip. Make sure a reliable person on shore knows your destination. Watch the weather; if it turns bad, head home or to a nearby shelter.

Know what to do in case of emergency. If the boat capsizes, stay with it. It will usually float, supporting you, until help arrives. Avoid taking nonswimmers in your boat, and always insist that children wear some sort of flotation devices even if they can swim.

Boating is fun, but it can be dangerous. A boat should always be operated with respect for the craft itself and for the water and weather conditions.

☐ Swimming

Many accidents and deaths occur each year during what for most of us is a wonderfully relaxing activity: swimming. Pool, lake, beach, ocean—each has its own appeal and its own dangers. You should be aware of the hazards and avoid them. Drowning or other serious accidents can happen without warning, and you should be alert to potential hazards.

POOLS

Swimming pools, particularly home pools, despite their clear water and seeming safety, have hazards of their own. Slippery walkways, decks, diving boards, and ladders can be hazardous and should be approached with care. Diving into unmarked shallow water is often the source of injury; swimming around protruding pipes can cause cuts and scrapes.

Most pool drownings occur among children under the age of five. A child should never be permitted to splash in a pool without constant adult supervision. A home pool should have a *locked* fence, 4 to 6 feet high, to keep children from wandering into the pool area.

NATURAL WATERS

Natural waters, such as lakes and oceans, present other hazards. Beware of undertows, fast currents, whirlpools, floating logs, and submerged rocks. If you feel strong currents, get out immediately. Watch for dangerous marine life, especially when swimming at unfamiliar beaches. Jellyfish, hydras, stinging fish, and other water life can give painful bites and stings.

White water is water mixed with air bubbles, usually resulting from waterfalls or water rushing over rocks. Such water is less buoyant than still water and more difficult to swim in. Avoid it.

CURRENTS

If you are caught in a current, do not attempt to fight it. Instead, swim directly across the current. Even though this may bring you further downstream, it will enable you to reach safety without becoming exhausted.

UNDERTOWS, RUNOUTS, AND RIP CURRENTS

Undertows, runouts, and rip currents tend to drag the swimmer away from the shore. Do not panic or struggle. Instead, swim parallel to shore across the current and, once free, swim to shore.

WATER RESCUE

If you swim often, you should be trained in water safety. Check your local Y or Red Cross center about lifesaving courses. Unless you are trained in lifesaving, do not attempt to rescue a drowning swimmer while you are in the water. You, too, may be pulled under. However, you can do the following:

From dock, raft, or poolside: Lie down and try to reach the drowning person with your hand, a shirt, a towel, or a pole to pull him to safety.

From the shore: Wade out into chest-high water. Get a good footing, grasp the victim's wrist, and then slowly move backward. If you can't reach the victim, push a board, ladder, or buoy to him to help him stay afloat.

From a boat: If you are in a motorboat, *shut off the engine* and move close to the victim, using oars or a paddle. Turn the boat so that the victim can grab the back or side of the boat. Stay seated and balance the boat as you pull him over the side. If you are near the shore, instruct the victim to cling to the back of the boat while you row to shore.

GENERAL SAFETY HINTS FOR SWIMMERS

Never swim after a large meal. Blood that is helping to digest your food is diverted from muscles, and you are apt to suffer cramps.

Learn to swim! It is unwise even to enter the water at a beach or pool without knowing how to swim. Never play in water unless you are a competent swimmer.

□ Bicycling

More and more people are bicycling to work, to school, for exercise, for fun, and for inexpensive, pollution-free transportation. However, because bicycles are lightweight, precarious vehicles and because traffic is sometimes heavy, bicycling can be dangerous. Most bicycle accidents occur because of careless riding or because of a defect in the bicycle.

ON THE ROAD

Four out of five bicycle accidents result from a disregard of traffic rules. Bikes should be driven as safely as any other road vehicle. In fact, the bicyclist is subject to the same rules as any other driver. You must, for example, stop at red lights and stop signs, give clear turn signals, and ride in single file in the right lane of the road.

Some special tips for bicyclists are:

- Ride near the curb in the same direction as traffic. Always ride in single file.

- Do not compete with high-speed, heavy traffic. Try to stay on less-traveled routes or bicycle paths.

- Do not clown on a bicycle.

- Be alert to road conditions, such as sewer grates, potholes, rocks, loose sand, and other surface problems. Avoid obstacles such as opening car doors and children jumping into the road.

- Avoid riding in bad weather, if possible. Wet tires tend to skid and wet handbrakes may slip. Visibility may be impaired.

- Keep all bicycle parts properly adjusted and in good condition. See that tires are properly inflated, and replace worn tires immediately. Replace all damaged or worn parts such as chain links, screws, bolts, seats, and brakes.

- Know all traffic laws and signals.

- Be extremely cautious at intersections; they are the site of most bicycle collisions with automobiles.

SELECTING A SAFE BICYCLE

When buying a bicycle, it is important to buy the most suitable—and the safest—bike for you. Look for the following:

- *A strong frame.* Improperly welded joints or cracks can cause the entire frame to give way in a sudden jolt.

- *No sharp edges.* If your bike has sharp edges or protrusions, file them down or cover them with tape.

- *Excellent brakes.* Brakes should stop quickly, smoothly, and easily. Test the brakes before you buy a bicycle. If you are buying a bike with handbrakes, be sure the levers move easily and are quickly accessible, particularly for children or adults with small hands.

- *A chain guard.* Clothing or shoelaces can catch in an exposed chain, causing serious accidents. In addition to a guard, consider using leg bands or trouser clips.

- *Reflectors.* Make sure you have front, rear, pedal, and spoke reflectors. You should also consider having reflecting sidewall tires, a headlight, and a taillight. You might attach reflectors to your clothing if you ride your bicycle at night.

- *Excellent tires.* Tires have two functions: to cushion the driver and to aid in braking. Tires should have good treads to enable the driver to ride smoothly and stop quickly.

- *Sufficient pedal clearance.* Pedals should not touch the ground when the bike is tilted less than 25 degrees. If they do, they may scrape on the ground during turns.

- *Proper fit.* The seat and handlebars should be adjusted to fit the rider comfortably. A man straddling the horizontal bar should have 1-inch clearance between the bar and his crotch when both feet are on the ground. A woman seated on the bike and with one leg on a pedal at its lowest position should be able to reach the ground with the ball of her other foot.

□ Skiing

Downhill skiing is an extremely hazardous sport, not only because of the speed built up in a downhill run, but because severe weather conditions and dangerous terrain are often part of the sport.

In general, for safe skiing, take lessons from an expert before starting off on your own. Know how to *turn well* and *stop safely* before tackling anything more than a novice-class slope. Take lessons occasionally as you perfect your skills to make sure you are executing turns the correct way to avoid strains, sprains, and fractures.

Dress for protection against the wind and cold. Wear a ski parka and flexible pants. Pay special attention to *socks* (you should wear a smooth inner pair and a heavy outer pair) and *gloves* (you should invest in proper ski gloves or mitts and wear a thin pair underneath). Be sure your head, and particularly your ears, are sufficiently protected. In extremely cold or windy weather, you should wear a face mask. If your eyes are sensitive, you might also invest in goggles.

GENERAL SAFETY HINTS FOR SKIERS

Never try to ski down a slope that is beyond your ability. Most slopes are marked according to their difficulty; pay attention to warning signs. Never stop in the middle of a run; look both ways before crossing a trail.

After a fall, fill in depressions made in the snow by your body and equipment. These holes and bumps are hazardous to other skiers. Keep safety straps secure so your skis don't escape. Keep your bindings free of dirt, salt, snow, and ice. Lubricate them frequently to reduce friction and prevent rust.

Get in good physical condition before going skiing. Don't overexert yourself at first; build up your endurance. Do a few warm-up exercises before you go out onto the slopes.

SPECIAL SAFETY TIPS ABOUT SKI EQUIPMENT

BOOTS
The fit of the boot is very important. If boots are too large, your feet can slip forward and impair your ability to control the skis. If they are too tight, they can restrict circulation and cause frostbite. Beginners should use a soft, low boot rather than the high boot often preferred by experts. High boots offer more stability and greater protection for the ankle, but they can cause severe leg injuries if you fall.

Your boots should be compatible with your bindings so that they do not interfere with the proper operation of the binding. To avoid a mismatch, take your boots along when you buy bindings. The ski mechanic will check them and make any necessary adjustments.

Use an antifriction device, such as a Teflon pad, between your ski and your boot sole. This reduces the friction on the ski and allows the binding mechanism to work freely.

Take particular care when fitting children with ski boots. Do not buy boots too large for your children, thinking that they can use extra socks until their feet grow. This is unsafe. Buy the right size. There are many places where you can trade children's ski boots for larger sizes as the children grow.

SKIS AND BINDINGS

Allow an expert to determine the proper skis for you. Ski length depends on your height, weight, and skill and on the type of snow you are planning to ski on. Since bindings match the boots, skis should be marked "left" and "right" and should not be interchanged.

The ski binding is the most critical part of the ski gear. It is designed to hold the skier's foot to the ski, yet when the skier loses control the binding must release him from the skis before he suffers a serious injury. At the same time, the binding should not release too easily, exposing the skier to injury from an unnecessary fall. The binding should have at least two releasing components: one triggered by a forward fall, the other triggered by twisting forces. As a rule, you should have the ski mechanic adjust the bindings to ensure proper interaction between the boot and the binding. Test your bindings from time to time to see if adjustment is needed.

To test your bindings at home:

For toe release—with the ski boot on and inserted into the binding, bend your knee forward and inward, thus trapping the inner edge of your ski. You should be able to release your toe with any further rotation of the lower part of your leg.

For heel release—with the ski flat on the floor and someone standing on the tail of the ski, step forward with the other leg (no ski) and pull the heel being tested upward so that your own muscle strength allows the heel to release.

About 40 percent of all ski injuries are caused by faulty bindings. Take care that yours work well.

☐ Sledding and tobogganing

Sledding seems a rather tame sport; yet the U.S. Consumer Product Safety Commission estimates that more than 34,000 people each year are treated for injuries associated with sleds, toboggans, snow disks, and snow tubes.

These accidents are usually the result of faulty equipment, less-than-adequate sledding conditions, loss of control, and collision.

For general safety while sledding, make sure you're using a vehicle that is in good condition. Beware of a sled made of flimsy materials, with splinters or protrusions, or not equipped with a flexible steering device. Avoid danger spots on slopes, such as bumps, tree stumps, rocks, ice, and bare spots. As a rule, sled on designated slopes in parks or winter recreation areas. Never slide through a traffic intersection or across a street. A car can come up suddenly, and the snowy road makes stopping difficult.

Do not slide until the slope is clear of other sledders. Move off the slope quickly when you reach the bottom. Walk to the top along a side path, out of the way of other sledders coming down.

To maintain your sled or toboggan, dry it off thoroughly before you put it away. Occasionally rub candlewax on the runners and other metal parts to make them slide smoothly and remain rust-free. Lubricate metal bolts, pivots, and rivets with a drop or two of oil. Sand down any rough or splintered parts. Wax the sled at the beginning of the season to make it waterproof.

☐ Snowmobiling

Snowmobiling is a relatively new and exciting winter sport, but it has also proved a fairly hazardous one. Each winter, many collisions (especially on public roads) are reported. These are often the result of driving too fast, riding on unfamiliar terrain, operating the snowmobile without proper instruction, and driving while intoxicated.

Before operating a snowmobile, become familiar with the vehicle. Always wear goggles, a helmet with chin straps, and warm protective clothing. Never wear a scarf or loose clothing that can catch in moving parts or on surrounding trees or shrubbery.

Know the traffic laws. Many states prohibit the use of snowmobiles on public roads and have minimum age requirements for snowmobile drivers.

Plan your route carefully. Watch the path ahead of you to avoid rocks, trees, fences, and other obstacles. Do not drive on an ice-covered pond or lake. You cannot tell the thickness of the ice just by sight. Avoid driving in bad weather; check the weather forecast before you go out.

Be alert at all times. The snowmobile's own noise may prevent you from hearing another approaching vehicle. Always stop before crossing a highway or railroad track.

A snowmobile, enjoyable as it is, is not a toy. Use it to have fun, but treat it with the same respect you would an automobile or a motorcycle.

☐ Ice skating

Ice skating appears to be a relatively mild and safe sport, but particularly on a stream, pond, or lake, the skater must use care to avoid drowning and other severe accident and injury. In judging the strength of ice on a pond, do not assume it is safe simply because it is thick in one spot. The ice may be strong in one place, but thin in another. If possible, skate only on a flooded field or shallow pond where water is only 1 or 2 feet deep.

In general, always be wary of the condition of the ice. Even at a skating rink, the ice may be rutted and rough and therefore hazardous to skaters. Never skate alone on an unfamiliar pond. Do not skate fast or race with others in crowded areas. If you are a beginner, stay in an area apart from experienced skaters.

Wear skates that fit properly and are sharp. When carrying skates, cover the blades with safety guards to protect not only the skates themselves, but yourself and others.

Appendix

Occupational Safety and Health Administration

For information regarding safety procedures and requirements *on the job,* write to an office of the United States Department of Labor in your region.

☐ Region I
(Connecticut, Maine, Massachusetts, New Hampshire, Rhode Island, Vermont)

Regional Office
18 Oliver Street
Boston, Massachusetts 02110

Area Offices
Custom House Building
State Street
Boston, Massachusetts 02109

450 Main Street
Room 617
Hartford, Connecticut 06103

55 Pleasant Street
Room 425
Concord, New Hampshire 03301

U.S. Courthouse
Room 503A
Providence, Rhode Island 02903

☐ Region II
(New Jersey, New York, Canal Zone, Puerto Rico, Virgin Islands)

Regional Office
1515 Broadway
New York, New York 10036

Area Offices
90 Church Street
Room 1405
New York, New York 10007

700 East Water Street
Room 203
Syracuse, New York 13210

370 Old Country Road
Garden City, New York 11530

970 Broad Street
Room 635
Newark, New Jersey 07102

605 Condado Avenue
Room 328
Santurce, Puerto Rico 00907

☐ Region III
(Delaware, District of Columbia, Maryland, Pennsylvania, Virginia, West Virginia)

Regional Office
15220 Gateway Center
3535 Market Street
Philadelphia, Pennsylvania 19104

Area Offices
1317 Filbert Street
Suite 1010
Philadelphia, Pennsylvania 19107

3661 Virginia Beach Boulevard
Room 111
Norfolk, Virginia 23502

400 North 8th Street
Room 8018
Richmond, Virginia 23240

31 Hopkins Plaza
Room 1110A
Baltimore, Maryland 21201

Jonnet Building
4099 William Penn Highway
Room 802
Monroeville, Pennsylvania 15146

☐ Region IV
(Alabama, Florida, Georgia,
Kentucky, Mississippi, North
Carolina, South Carolina,
Tennessee)

Regional Office
1375 Peachtree Street, NE
Suite 587
Atlanta, Georgia 30309

Area Offices
1371 Peachtree Street, NE
Room 723
Atlanta, Georgia 30309

3200 East Oakland Park Boulevard
Room 204
Fort Lauderdale, Florida 33308

2809 Art Museum Drive
Suite 4
Jacksonville, Florida 32207

600 Federal Place
Room 561
Louisville, Kentucky 40202

118 North Royal Street
Room 801
Mobile, Alabama 35502

1361 East Morehead Street
Charlotte, North Carolina 28204

1600 Hayes Street
Suite 302
Nashville, Tennessee 37203

2047 Canyon Road
Todd Mall
Birmingham, Alabama 35216

6605 Abercorn Street
Suite 201
Savannah, Georgia 31405

☐ Region V
(Illinois, Indiana, Michigan,
Minnesota, Ohio, Wisconsin)

Regional Office
300 South Wacker Drive
Room 1201
Chicago, Illinois 60606

Area Offices
300 South Wacker Drive
Chicago, Illinois 60606

700 Bryden Road
Room 224
Columbus, Ohio 43215

633 West Wisconsin Avenue
Room 500
Milwaukee, Wisconsin 53203

46 East Ohio Street
Room 423
Indianapolis, Indiana 45204

1240 East Ninth Street
Room 847
Cleveland, Ohio 44199

220 Bagley Avenue
Room 626
Detroit, Michigan 48225

110 South Fourth Street
Room 437
Minneapolis, Minnesota 55401

550 Main Street
Room 5522
Cincinnati, Ohio 45202

234 North Summit Street
Room 734
Toledo, Ohio 43504

☐ Region VI
(Arkansas, Louisiana, New Mexico, Oklahoma, Texas)

Regional Office
1512 Commerce Street
7th Floor
Dallas, Texas 75201

Area Offices
1100 Commerce Street
Room 601
Dallas, Texas 75202

1204 Texas Avenue
Room 421
Lubbock, Texas 79401

420 South Boulder
Room 512
Tulsa, Oklahoma 74103

307 Central National Bank Building
Houston, Texas 77002

546 Carondelet Street
4th Floor
New Orleans, Louisiana 70130

U.S. Customhouse Building
Room 3245
Galveston, Texas 77550

☐ Region VII
(Iowa, Kansas, Missouri, Nebraska)

Regional Office
823 Walnut Street
Room 300
Kansas City, Missouri 64106

Area Offices
1627 Main Street
Room 1100
Kansas City, Missouri 64108

210 North 12th Boulevard
Room 554
Saint Louis, Missouri 63101

City National Bank Building
Harney and 16th Streets
Room 803
Omaha, Nebraska 68102

☐ Region VIII
(Colorado, Montana, North Dakota, South Dakota, Utah, Wyoming)

Regional Office
1961 Stout Street
Room 15010
Denver, Colorado 80205

Area Offices
8527 West Colfax Avenue
Lakewood, Colorado 80215

455 East 4th South
Suite 309
Salt Lake City, Utah 84111

2812 First Avenue North
Suite 525
Billings, Montana 59101

☐ Region IX
(Arizona, California, Hawaii, Nevada, American Samoa, Guam, Trust Territory of the Pacific Islands)

Regional Office
450 Golden Gate Avenue
Room 9470
San Francisco, California 94102

Area Offices
100 McAllister Street
Room 1706
San Francisco, California 94102

2721 North Central Avenue
Suite 910
Phoenix, Arizona 85004

19 Pine Avenue
Room 514
Long Beach, California 90802

333 Queen Street
Suite 505
Honolulu, Hawaii 96813

☐ Region X
(Alaska, Idaho, Oregon,
Washington)

Regional Office
506 Second Avenue
Room 1808
Seattle, Washington 98104

Area Offices
506 Second Avenue
Room 1906
Seattle, Washington 98104

610 C Street
Room 214
Anchorage, Alaska 99501

921 SW Washington Street
Room 526
Portland, Oregon 97205

United States Consumer Product Safety Commission

The U.S. Consumer Product Safety Commission (CPSC) was established in 1973 to inform the public about the comparative safety of consumer products and to serve as a government agency for consumer complaints. If you would like further information about a product or wish to register a complaint about a product, call or write the commission's central office in Washington, D.C., or the regional office in your area.

☐ Central office

U.S. Consumer Product Safety Commission
Office of Communications
Washington, D.C. 20207
(800) 638-2566 (toll-free)

☐ Area offices

Atlanta
1330 West Peachtree Street, NW
Atlanta, Georgia 30309
(404) 526-2231

Boston
100 Summer Street
Room 1607
Boston, Massachusetts 02110
(617) 223-5576

Chicago
230 South Dearborn Street
Room 2945
Chicago, Illinois 60604
(312) 353-8260

Cleveland
Plaza Nine Building
55 Erieview Plaza
Room 520
Cleveland, Ohio 44114
(216) 522-3886

Dallas
500 South Ervay
Room 410 C
Dallas, Texas 75201
(214) 749-3871

Denver
Guaranty Bank Building
817 17th Street
Suite 938
Denver, Colorado 80202
(303) 837-2904

Kansas City
Traders National Bank Building
1125 Grand Avenue
Suite 1500
Kansas City, Missouri 64106
(816) 374-2034

Los Angeles
3660 Wilshire Boulevard
Suite 1100
Los Angeles, California 90010
(213) 688-7272

Minneapolis
Federal Building
Fort Snelling
Room 650
Twin Cities, Minnesota 55111
(612) 725-3424

New York
6th Floor
6 World Trade Center
Vesey Street
New York, New York 10048
(212) 264-1125

Philadelphia
400 Market Street
10th Floor
Philadelphia, Pennsylvania 19106
(215) 597-9105

San Francisco
100 Pine Street
Suite 500
San Francisco, California 94111
(415) 556-1816

Seattle
3240 Federal Building
915 Second Avenue
Seattle, Washington 98174
(206) 442-5276

Index